THE
GIANT JOKE BOOK

THE
GIANT JOKE BOOK

THE GIANT JOKE BOOK

by David Allen Clark

A Doubleday Fatback

Doubleday & Company, Inc.

Garden City, New York

Library of Congress Cataloging in Publication Data

Clark, David Allen.
　The giant joke book.

　SUMMARY: Contains hundreds of jokes and riddles.
　1. American wit and humor.　2. Wit and humor,
juvenile.　[1. Jokes.　2. Riddles]　I. Title.
PN6163.C58　　818'.5407
Library of Congress Catalog Card Number 80-2242
ISBN: 0-385-14721-X　Trade Paperback

Copyright © 1981 by Doubleday & Company, Inc.
All Rights Reserved
Printed in the United States of America
First Edition

CONTENTS

Just Jokes	1
Things That Go Bump in the Night	145
Knock Knock Jokes	157
Brushing With the Law	195
Healthy Jokes	205
Riddles, Riddles, Riddles!	225
Jokes in Verse	297
School Days, School Days	303
Daffynitions	341
The Wheels of Commerce	349
Elephants Bringing Up the Rear	373

Just Jokes

WILBUR: If two rights don't make a wrong, what do two rights make?
ORVILLE: An airplane?

A man walked into a room of the house he was visiting and found a boy playing chess with a dog.

"How remarkable!" said the man. "This is the most fantastic thing I have ever seen."

"He's not so great," replied the boy. "I've beaten him three out of the last five games."

A man walked into a bar. As he sat down, a bear, who was quite obviously the bartender, asked him what he would have. The man was quite startled and very disturbed. He could hardly compose himself enough to ask for a beer.

"What's the matter, pal," asked the bear, "is something bothering you?"

"Oh no, I'll be alright," replied the man, "I just didn't know the giraffe sold the place."

And then there was the guy who ate a whole jar of mustard because somebody told him he was full of baloney.

An Eskimo won a trip to New York as a prize for catching the most seals in a season. When he returned home, he brought with him a length of pipe, which he set up in his igloo so that it protruded through the roof.

His wife asked what it was for, and he said:

"That's a trick I learned in New York. When you want more heat, you bang on this pipe."

Did you hear about the scientist who worked with space problems so long that his head was full of it?

CLARA: What do you think of my dachshund?
ROSE: I never sausage a dog.

A mother pigeon was exasperated with one of her squabs, which was afraid of flying. The mother laid down an ultimatum: "Either you learn to fly today or I'll tie a string on you and drag you behind me."
"But, Mother," protested the little bird. "I don't want to be pigeon-towed."

STREET SPEAKER: We must get rid of radicalism, communism, socialism, and anarchism.
VOICE FROM THE CROWD: And while you're at it, how about rheumatism?

GEORGE: What kinds of wood make a match?
LARRY: That's easy. He would and she would.

CAL: I think I saw your wife downtown today. She was trying to park between two big trucks.

HAL: Did she make it?
CAL: Yes.
HAL: Then it wasn't my wife.

HUSBAND: It says here in the paper that if you peel onions under water, they won't make you cry.
WIFE: Well, if you think I'm going to become a scuba diver just to peel onions, you're nuts.

COWBOY: Do you want a horn on your saddle?
DUDE: No. There doesn't seem to be much traffic out here.

In the days of King Arthur and the Knights of the Round Table it was the custom to give shelter to wandering knights. On one stormy, rainy night, a knight, riding a huge shaggy dog, knocked on the door of a castle.

"Would you give shelter to a knight?" he asked.

"Of course," answered a voice from inside the castle, "I wouldn't turn a knight out on a dog like this."

Several high-ranking government officials of a new, developing country were flying in an airplane on an inspection tour. They flew over a plantation field and saw hundreds of people working the fields with primitive tools.

"Just think how happy they would be if I threw a dozen new tractors down to them," said the Minister of Agriculture.

"Just think how happy they would be if I dropped all the money they needed down onto them," said the Minister of Finance.

"Just think how happy they would be if I threw you down there," said the Minister of Justice to the Prime Minister.

HARRY: What's about six inches long, has a purple body with red spots, sixteen legs, four orange wings, four big biting pincers, eight glowing eyes, a forked tongue, and drools sticky stuff out of its mouth?

CLARA: I don't know. What?

HARRY: I don't know either, but whatever it is, it's on the back of your neck.

You've heard about those experts who can tell the sex of a day-old baby chick? Not too many people know how they do it, but one theory is they throw some corn to the chick. If he eats it the chick is a male, if she eats it the chick is a female.

WEATHER REPORT: Fifty per cent chance of rain.

TRANSLATION: Well, it might rain. But then again, it might not.

Two men went into the clothing business. They ordered goods and found on the invoice listings such as:
Dresses: size 6
    ″   ″ 8
    ″   ″ 10

One partner looked at the invoice and said, "What are those little marks?"

"I don't know," said the other partner.

"Go to the dress manufacturer and find out."

The partner went to the manufacturer and came back about an hour later.

"Well, what did you find out?"

"The mark is called a 'ditto.'"

"What does that mean?"

"It means what you are."

"What do you mean by that?"

"The dress manufacturer said that I'm an idiot and you're a ditto."

GREG: My uncle went horseback riding and now he's a mental case.

SUZY: From horseback riding?

GREG: Yeah. He has to eat off the mantel.

STU: Did you hear about big Olaf?

LOU: What about him?

STU: He was killed.

LOU: Killed! How?

STU: He was killed by a weasel.

LOU: A little thing like a weasel killed a big guy like Olaf?

STU: Yeah. He was walking along the railroad track and he didn't hear the weasel.

A one-ring circus was visiting a town in the hills. The folks recognized all the instruments of the band except for the slide trombone. One old fellow watched the player for quite some time, then said: "There's a trick to it. He ain't really swallerin' it."

A long-suffering wife was complaining to her husband about the state of her wardrobe.

"I haven't a decent thing to wear," she said tearfully. "If anybody new came over, they'd think I was the cook."

"Not," said her husband, "if they stayed for dinner."

The easiest way to tell the difference between valuable plants and weeds is to pull up everything. Then, if they come up again, they're weeds.

Anyone who thinks that the younger generation isn't creative should watch a teen-ager build a sandwich.

Science is wonderful. Scientists couldn't pry open a train window, so they air-conditioned the train.

A little boy was raking leaves with his father, who was telling him about what made leaves turn brown. Suddenly the little boy said: "What's all this about Jack Frost turning the leaves brown? Hasn't anyone ever heard of photosynthesis?"

NEIGHBOR: You've been working out in the garden all day. What are you growing?
SECOND NEIGHBOR: Tired.

UNCLE: What would you like to be when you grow up?
NEPHEW: A vitamin.
UNCLE: How can you be a vitamin?
NEPHEW: I don't know, but I saw a sign in the drugstore window that said, "Vitamin be one."

The boss was walking through the shipping room of his company when he noticed a young man sitting on top of a large box, whistling, and obviously not working.

"I'm angry, young man," he said. "What's your salary?"

"One hundred dollars a week, sir."

"Well, here's a week's pay. Now get out—you're fired."

When the boss saw the shipping room foreman later, he asked, "That good-for-nothing who was lolling around earlier—how long had he been with us?"

"That kid? He didn't work here, sir. He was just delivering a package."

Sign on a space pilot's door: "Out to Launch."

MOE: Hey! This match won't light.
HAL: What's the matter with it?
MOE: I don't know. It worked alright a few minutes ago.

SMITH: So that distinguished-looking gentleman in the tall hat is your leading citizen. Has he received many degrees from college?
JONES: Has he! Why, he has received so many degrees we call him the Human Thermometer.

An old farmer left his secluded farm for the first time in forty years to go to town and buy a new plow. In the hardware store he saw something he had never seen before, an electric fan. He stared for a moment at the whirling fan and said to the hardware man, "Boy, that's a fast squirrel you have in that cage."

ELLEN: What would you have done if you had discovered electricity?
CAROL: I'd have been too shocked to do anything.

For some time, the airline had given its passengers sticks of chewing gum labeled "To prevent unpleasant pressure in your ears during takeoff and landing."
It just *had* to happen. A passenger appealed to the flight attendant. "Help me get this stuff out of my ears. It doesn't help anyway."

VISITOR: All the mechanical toys you make seem to be very successful.
INVENTOR: Yes. I've had only one failure.
VISITOR: What was the matter with it?
INVENTOR: Too lifelike. It was a toy loafer and it wouldn't work.

A man walked into a New York travel agency and asked for a ticket to Chicago.
"Do you want to go by Buffalo?" asked the agent.
"Goodness no!" the man said. "If I can't go by train, let me have a reindeer."

HUSBAND (phoning his wife from the office): I've got two tickets for the theater.

WIFE: Wonderful. I'll start dressing.
HUSBAND: Yes, do. The tickets are for tomorrow night.

A university is an institution with room for twenty thousand people in the classrooms and eighty thousand in the stadium.

LES: Don't worry, that's only a little green snake.
LINDA: Yes, but maybe it's just as dangerous as a ripe one.

A small planet broke out of its orbit and raced around the sun and the moon. The mother planet called out, "Junior, what out of this world are you doing?"
The smaller planet raced toward her and said, "Look, Mom—no gravities."

CRAIG: I was shot through the leg.
JUDY: Have a scar?
CRAIG: No thanks. I don't smoke.

A mouse was putting up a knotty pine wall in his living room. A smaller mouse came along and said, "What are those holes for?"
"They're knotholes," said the bigger mouse.
"Well then," said the smaller mouse, "if they're not holes, what are they?"

All a wallflower needs to blossom out on dates is some son.

A man was defeated for the office of sheriff in a western town. The next day, he was seen walking down the street with a gun on his hip.
Friend: "Don't you know you weren't elected sheriff and you have no right to wear a gun?"
The man answered, "In the election I got thirty-five votes out of three thousand. A man who doesn't have any more friends than I have needs to carry a gun."

The motorist had had an accident. His car had run over a man's toes, and the victim was claiming damages. "What?" said the motorist. "You want one million dollars for a damaged foot? I'm not a millionaire."
"Maybe you aren't," said the victim. "But I'm not a centipede."

CHARLOTTE: So your husband is one of the big guns of industry?
JANET: Yes. He's been fired seven times.

FIRST SCIENTIST: We have finally discovered an acid that will eat up everything.
SECOND SCIENTIST: What are we going to keep it in?

PRISCILLA: Have you heard I'm engaged to an Irish boy?
LUCY: Oh, really?
PRISCILLA: No. O'Reilly.

A county agent from an agricultural school was telling a farmer how he could make his farm more profitable and keep it in better condition.

Finally the farmer said, "Listen here, young man, these newfangled ideas of yours don't impress me at all. You can't tell me how to run a farm. I've worn out three of them already."

SEAMAN: A woman fell overboard yesterday from a passing ship and we were horrified a few minutes later to see a shark swimming toward her.
PASSENGER: Did he seize her?
SEAMAN: No. He just swam up to her, took a look, and swam away.
PASSENGER: Why?
SEAMAN: He was a man-eating shark.

An alarmed motorist stopped hurriedly when he saw a young man standing beside an overturned sports car. "Anybody hurt in the accident?" he asked.

"There wasn't any accident," said the young man. "I'm changing a tire."

AUNT SUSIE: That's a comet.
EDDIE: A what?
AUNT SUSIE: A comet, Eddie. Don't you know what a comet is?
EDDIE: No.
AUNT SUSIE: Don't you know what they call a star with a tail?
EDDIE: Sure. Mickey Mouse.

Two fathers, whose sons were students at Yale and Harvard, respectively, frequently compared notes on the progress of the young men as shown by their letters home.

"Claude's letters always send me to the dictionary," said one.

"You're lucky," said the other. "My boy's letters always send me to the bank."

A young sailor who had lost his rifle was brought before the commander and told he would have to pay for his weapon.

"Suppose I'd lost a launch. Would I have to pay for that?"

"Yes, even if it took the rest of your navy career to do it," answered the commander.

"Now I understand why the captain goes down with his ship."

FIRST TEXAN: Heard you bought another new Cadillac.

SECOND TEXAN: Almost had to. I ducked into their showroom to make a phone call and didn't like to leave without buying something.

The weatherman had been wrong so often in his predictions that he had become the laughingstock of the town. When the teasing became unbearable, he asked for a transfer.
"Why?" wrote headquarters, "do you wish to be transferred to another station?"
"Because," the man wrote back, "the climate here doesn't agree with me."

GRACE: Did you hear the story about the mountain?
RORY: No, I didn't.
GRACE: It's all a bluff.

It was hunting season when a state trooper walked up to a man and his son and said, "That's a nice buck you have on the front of your car. And that's your limit."
The surprised man couldn't say anything, so his son said, "That's nothing, you should see the one we have in the trunk."

An Australian sheep farmer, having drawn a huge check from the sale of wool, bought a luxurious limousine. When he brought it back for servicing, the salesman asked if he was satisfied.

"Oh yes," said the farmer. "I especially like that glass partition between the front seat and the back. Keeps the sheep out of the front seat."

The little boy sat before the fireplace stroking his new kitten. When it suddenly began to purr loudly, the boy jerked it roughly away from the hearth. "Can't you treat your new pet more gently?" his mother asked.

"But, Mom," the little boy said. "I had to move it fast. Didn't you hear it starting to boil?"

It takes approximately three thousand bolts to put an automobile together but only one nut to scatter it all over the highway.

EUNICE: Is your boyfriend lazy?
CLAUDETTE: Is he! Why, when he wants to brush his teeth, he holds a toothbrush in front of him and watches a tennis match.

TOM: It couldn't have rained all the time you were on vacation—you're all sunburned.
PAT: Sunburn nothing. That's rust.

Two buckets met each other in the street. "You're a little pail," said one.

"Yes," replied the other. "I'm not a well bucket."

Two granddaughters became intrigued with a small turtle in a bowl. One morning they went to see him and he had gone into his shell. "Come quickly, Grandma!" the older girl screamed. "The turtle has gone and has forgotten to take his umbrella with him."

Once there was a mamma skunk and a little skunk named Moe. One day Moe asked his mother for a chemistry set. "No," she said. "You'll smell up the house."

A boy was finishing his report to the class on jet aviation. "Our modern flyers can do anything that a bird can do, and more," he announced proudly.
From a corner of the room, another boy whispered, "I'd like to see one of them lay an egg."

LITTLE BOY: Daddy, what makes it rain?
FATHER: I don't know much about weather, son.
LITTLE BOY: How does television work, Dad?
FATHER: I'm afraid electronics is just not my thing.
LITTLE BOY: How do whales breathe?

FATHER: I don't know.
LITTLE BOY: Dad, am I bothering you with all these questions?
FATHER: Of course not. How do you expect to learn anything if you don't ask questions?

TRUDY: I'm disgusted.
LISA: Why?
TRUDY: I stepped on a scale today and a card came out that said, "One person at a time, please."

FATHER: You're a pig. Do you know what a pig is?
SON: Yes, Dad. A pig is a hog's little boy.

VOICE ON THE PHONE: Are you the game warden?
GAME WARDEN: Yes, I am.
VOICE: Would you please give me some suggestions for a child's birthday party?

PROFESSOR: I say there, you in the automobile. Your tubular air container has lost its rotundity.
MOTORIST: What?
PROFESSOR: I said the cylindrical apparatus which supports your vehicle is no longer symmetrical.
MOTORIST: Who?
PROFESSOR: The elastic fabric surrounding the

circular frame whose successive revolutions bear you onward in space has not retained its pristine nature.

MOTORIST: Which?

PASSING BOY: Mister, he says you have a flat tire.

HE: Do you know her to speak to?
SHE: No. Only to talk about.

A newspaper plastered this headline over a news story concerning a new development in the H-bomb situation: "U.S. Finding Way to Cut Fall-Out."

The paper was hardly on the street when a caller contacted the city desk. "If they cut fall out, does that mean we are going to go from summer right into winter?"

"I gave that man a half-dollar for saving my life."
"What did he do?"
"He gave me back twenty cents change."

"So your uncle was a conductor. Railroad or orchestra?"
"Neither. He was struck by lightning."

A sugar planter in Hawaii told a visitor that a certain volcano was 90,006 years old. The visitor said, "I'm amazed. I can understand how it might be estimated at approximately ninety thousand years old, but how do you arrive at exactly ninety thousand and six years?"

The planter said, "Well, they told me that the volcano was ninety thousand years old when I moved here six years ago."

WEATHER BUREAU FORECASTER (to assistant): Shut the windows when you leave the office. You never can tell when it's going to rain.

The cranky old lady was angry because her neighbors had not asked her to a picnic. On the morning of the picnic, one of them called to ask her to go along. "It's too late," she snapped. "I've already prayed for rain."

A cameraman working for the education department of a film company met an old farmer in town and said, "I've just been taking some moving pictures of life on your farm."

"Did you catch any of my hired hands in motion?"

"Yes."

"Ain't science wonderful!"

One morning Grimes looked over his garden wall and said to his neighbor: "What are you burying in that hole?"

"Oh," said the neighbor. "I'm just replanting some of my seeds."

"Seeds!" shouted Grimes angrily. "It looks more like one of my hens."

The neighbor answered, "It is. My seeds are inside her."

DAN: It's a good thing that adults split atoms.
STAN: Why?
DAN: If we did it, they'd make us put them back together.

FIRST NEIGHBOR: What are all of your chickens doing out in front of the house?
SECOND NEIGHBOR: They heard that some men were going to lay a sidewalk and they wanted to see how it was done.

JIM: Mr. Kelly left his umbrella again. I believe he'd leave his head if it were loose.
SLIM: You're right. I heard him say yesterday that he is going to Arizona for his lungs.

MOTHER: How can I keep a jar of cookies hidden from the kids?
FATHER: Lock the jar and hide the key under a bar of soap.

MILLY: You're pretty dirty, Trudy.
TRUDY: Yes, and I'm even prettier clean.

LADY: What can I do for you?
BUM: I have a button. Would you sew a coat on it?

BRUCE: They say that paper can be used to keep a person warm.
CHARLIE: You're telling me. I once owned a mortgage that kept me sweating for twenty years.

PASSENGER: You know it takes courage for me to take this flight. I was almost killed twice in a plane.
PILOT: Once would have been enough.

DAIRYMAN: This is the latest type of milking machine.
CITY LADY: But do you think any of these machines make as good milk as cows do?

FARMER: Young feller, you're brave to come down in a parachute in an awful cyclone like this.
YOUNG MAN: I didn't come down in a parachute. I went up in a tent.

VISITOR: Can you tell me where the science building is?
COLLEGE BOY: I'm sorry. I can't. I'm just here on a football scholarship.

JEZEBEL: My uncle disappeared while he was on a bear-hunting trip.
MAX: What happened to him?
JEZEBEL: Something he disagreed with ate him.

BOY SCOUT: May I accompany you across the street, madam?
ELDERLY LADY: Certainly, sonny. How long have you been waiting here for someone to help you across?

SMALL GIRL (showing a scale to a playmate): All I know is that you stand on it and it makes you mad.

Asked if fertilizer would stimulate a certain plant's growth, the farmer replied: "Can't say for sure. I've never been able to understand whether the stuff actually stimulates the plants or whether it's just so downright repulsive that they try to grow away from it."

"The scientists say that the inside of the earth isn't as hot as was thought."
"No, and neither is the outside."

HUSBAND: It says here in the paper that in order to make a teaspoonful of honey, a bee must visit two thousand flowers.

WIFE: Well, I'll bet that someday some smart farmer is going to give them the spoonful and save all that wear and tear on his bees.

RICK: What's the name of those tablets the ancient Gauls used to write on?
MICK: Gaul stones.

GLEN: My trained flea is all tired out.
FRAN: Why?
GLEN: He must have been on a tramp all week.

ALEX: Did you ever do any public speaking?
FRED: Yes. Once I proposed to a girl in the country over a party line.

WIFE: It says here in the paper that some trees drink two hundred gallons of water a day.
HUSBAND: Well, no wonder willows weep.

OUR LATEST INVENTION: A clock without hands for people who don't care what time it is.

One of the best marksmen of the FBI was passing through a small town. Everywhere he saw evidence of the most amazing shooting. On trees, on walls, and on fences there were numerous bull's-eyes with the bullet hole in the absolute center. The FBI man asked to meet the person responsible for this wonderful marksmanship. The man turned out to be the village idiot.

"This is the best marksmanship I've ever seen," the FBI man said. "How in the world do you do it?"

"Easy as pie," said the idiot. "I shoot first and draw the circles afterward."

SAM: A pessimist takes the worst possible view of things.
STAN: That's not a pessimist. That's an amateur photographer.

VISITOR TO RANCHER: What's that rope on your saddle for?
RANCHER: Catching cows.
VISITOR: How interesting. What do you use for bait?

Few children naturally fear water unless soap is added.

JENNY: I hear that your brother had an accident in the submarine service.
LENNY: Yes. He never got over the habit of opening the windows each night when he went to bed. And one night . . .

HELEN: Did you hear about the two blood cells?

LEE: No. What happened?
HELEN: They loved in vein.

MAN (on airplane trip): As I contemplate the wonders of nature from high in the sky, I realize how insignificant man really is.
WOMAN: Humph! A woman can see that without going up in a plane.

FIRST SAILOR: Why didn't you volunteer for submarine duty?
SECOND SAILOR: I didn't want anything to do with a ship that sinks on purpose.

SERGEANT: Private, did your nurse drop you on your head when you were a baby?
RECRUIT: No. We couldn't afford a nurse. My mother had to do it.

After failing for the second time to pass his road test required for an operator's license, the young man admitted that traffic bothered him.
"Well," questioned the sympathetic officer, "why not wait a year or so and try again?"
"But I can't," said the disappointed man. "You see, I have to get back and forth to the airport. I'm a pilot."

FIRST BOY: I've been experimenting with electricity.

SECOND BOY: What did you get?
FIRST BOY: Shocking results.

KATHY: Did you hear about the hen that swallowed a Yo-Yo?
JAY: No, what happened?
KATHY: She laid the same egg three times.

MAVIS: Did you hear about the fish that had the measles?
TRAVIS: No. How's he doing?
MAVIS: Pretty well. He just had them on a small scale.

GUIDE: I saw a lot of tiger tracks just north of here.
NEW HUNTER: Good! Which way is south?

The Scouts were discussing their coming camping trip. "What would you do if a bear came after you while you were out in the woods?" Al asked Jim.

"I'd climb a tree," Jim answered.

"But bears climb trees too," Al answered.

"Not this tree." Jim laughed. "It would be shaking too much."

FIRST MOUNTAIN CLIMBER: Have you heard the rumor about old Sir Treadway, the intrepid mountain climber?

SECOND MOUNTAIN CLIMBER: No. What?
FIRST MOUNTAIN CLIMBER: He's past his peak.

A scientist was applying for an important job at Cape Kennedy. Following a series of security clearances and written tests, he was interviewed by the personnel manager. "Give me three reasons why you think you should have this position," said the hiring chief.
"Certainly," said the applicant. "Third, I have the necessary technical qualifications. Second, my temperament is suited to the work. And first, I know how to count."

The astronomy professor was lecturing. "I predict the end of the world in fifty million years."
"How many?" cried a frightened voice from the audience.
"Fifty million years."
"Oh," said the voice with relief. "I thought you said fifteen million."

When we were kids, fifteen cents was considered big money. How dimes have changed.

LOUIS: My uncle is so rich that he has an electric fan in every room.
STEWART: That's nothing. My uncle is so rich

he hires a helicopter to hover over his house and cool the entire neighborhood.

MELANIE: Do you think there is any intelligent life on Mars?
DAVE: There must be. You don't see them spending thirty billion dollars to come here, do you?

While visiting London, a Texan was bragging about how big everything was in Texas. A London man got angry and put a two-hundred-pound turtle in the Texan's bed. The Texan ran out of his room yelling, "There's something in my room!"
The London man said, "I see you found one of our bedbugs."

VISITOR TO AN AIR FORCE BASE: Oh, do your planes leak?
PILOT: Yes, madam. We carry parachutes in case we have to bail out.

LIL: Why did they name you Bill?
BILL: I came on the first of the month.

APPLICANT: So this apartment was occupied by an experimental scientist. I suppose that those spots on the wall are from his experiments.
LANDLADY: No. Those spots are the scientist.

One termite met another termite in front of a wooden venetian blind. "Look, Morton," said the first. "Our bread is coming sliced now."

LATE-STAYER: I can imitate any bird.
WEARY HOSTESS: How about a homing pigeon?

SCIENTIST: We can get rain by spraying the clouds.
SCIENTIST'S WIFE: All I have to do to bring rain is to wash the windows.

"Do you have cold winters in Arkansas?"
"No, but we have Hot Springs."

FLORA: I've owned this car for eight years and never had a wreck.
HARRY: What you mean is that you've owned this wreck for eight years and never had a car.

SKIP: Mom, I need a new jacket.
MOTHER: Skip, your horsehide jacket is only a month old and nearly worn out?
SKIP: Yes, Mom, but look how long the horse wore it.

A mother moth was surprised to find her baby moth crying. "Stop that at once," she commanded. "This is the first time I ever saw a moth bawl."

LADY: Mister, your car is smoking.
DRIVER: Lady, it's old enough.

EDITOR (to contributor): Did you write these poems yourself?
POET: Yes, sir. Right out of my head.
EDITOR: You must be.

A bride of a few weeks greeted her husband with a happy smile. "Well, dear," she said, "your dinner is going to be different tonight. A neighbor told me that you are supposed to add water to dehydrated foods."

"Do you realize," said a man in a cafeteria to a stranger across the table, "that you are reading your newspaper upside down?"
"Of course I realize it," snapped the stranger. "Do you think it's easy?"

FIRST DOG: My name is Rover. What's yours?
SECOND DOG: I'm not sure, but I think it's Down Boy.

STEVE: I read in the newspaper that a man ate ten dozen pancakes.
PAM: Oh, how waffle!

A group of Boy Scouts were sitting around a fire. One boy said, "We'd better go to bed before the mosquitoes eat us up."

Late that night the boy looked out of his tent and saw some fireflies. He quickly woke up his friend and said, "We'd better hide. They're coming after us with flashlights."

Some people are like fences. They run around a lot but never get anywhere.

ANN: You say that you can spell the longest word in the English language?
CONRAD: S-M-I-L-E-S.
ANN: But that word has only six letters.
CONRAD: Yes. But there's a mile between the first and last letters.

A sailor rushed up to the officer on the deck in such excitement that he stammered and stuttered. The officer lost patience with him and said, "Sing it out, sailor, sing it out!"
The sailor drew a deep breath and began to sing, "Should auld acquaintance be forgot and never brought to mind? The admiral's fallen overboard, he's half a mile behind."

SHEILA: Pug was put in jail for stealing a pig.
STAN: How could they prove he did it?
SHEILA: The pig squealed.

Too many girls think a woman's work is done when she sweeps down the aisle.

It was the first time that he had taken his girl friend fishing. After a few minutes with their lines in the water, she asked, "What did that red and white thing on my line cost?"

"The bobber?" he asked. "Oh, about twenty-five cents. Why?"

"Well, I owe you twenty-five cents, because mine just sank."

PAM: How did you like the play last night?
RON: The first act was wonderful, but I didn't stay for the second act.
PAM: Why not?
RON: I couldn't wait that long. It said on the program, "two years later."

FRED: Did you hear about the guy who stayed up all night figuring out where the sun went when it went down?
GERT: No. What happened?
FRED: It finally dawned on him.

PHIL: Why do they figure the electric bill in kilowatts?
HANS: Because you pay for all those watts that were killed as they went through the meter.

One day two white mice were talking with each other through the bars of their laboratory cages. One, looking up, noticed a white-frocked scientist advancing upon the cage and carrying a huge hypodermic needle. "Oh no," groaned the mouse. "Here comes that man with his needle again. He makes me sick!"

SON: Dad, are you growing taller all the time?
FATHER: No. Why do you ask?
SON: Because the top of your head is poking through your hair.

Parents spend the first part of a child's life urging him to walk and talk, and the rest of his childhood making him sit down and keep quiet.

GRANDSON: Grandma, get off the stove.
GRANDMOTHER: Why?
GRANDSON: You're too old to be riding the range.

MOTHER: Where are you going, Valerie?
VALERIE: I'm going out to watch a solar eclipse.
MOTHER: Alright, darling, but don't stand too close.

BOY (to older man): Would you please open the gate for me?
OLDER MAN: Why, of course, sonny.
BOY: Thanks. It was just painted, and I didn't want to get my hands messy.

Did you hear about the schoolteacher who fell into the copying machine and came out beside herself?

JUD (sitting at the dinner table): Even though it looks like there are only two chickens on that platter, I can prove that there are really three chickens there.
FATHER: Alright. Go ahead.
JUD (pointing at one chicken): This is one. Right?
FATHER: Yes.
JUD (pointing at the other chicken): And this is two. OK?
FATHER: Yes.
JUD: So don't one and two make three?
FATHER: Fine. I'll serve myself the first chicken, your mother the second, and you can have the third.

BOB: If I saw a man beating a donkey and made him stop, what virtue would I be showing?
HAL: Brotherly love.

After a morning of playing outdoors, little Harry came into the house.
HARRY: Who am I?
MOTHER: Let's see . . . The Incredible Hulk?
HARRY: I guess Mrs. Smith was right. She said

I was so dirty that my own mother wouldn't recognize me.

DAD (looking suspiciously at the dessert his daughter has just whipped up): What's this?
DAUGHTER: It's cottage pudding. We learned how to make it at school today.
DAD: Well, I think I got a piece of shingle in my mouth.

JEAN: I've just swallowed a great big worm.
JOE: Hadn't you better take something for it?
JEAN: No. Let it starve.

In the mood for joking, a vacationing sportsman stopped when he saw a farmer working in a field and asked: "Did you happen to see a wagonload of monkeys go by here?"
"No," replied the farmer. "Did you fall off?"

MIKE: What makes you think that Atlas was a bad man?
GAIL: Because it says in this book that he held up the whole world.

PROUD MOTHER: Baby is a year old now and he has been walking since he was eight months old.
BORED VISITOR: Really? He must be awfully tired.

PHYLLIS: Does the giraffe get a wet throat when he gets wet feet?
CONNIE: Yes, but not until the next week.

JACK: What are you doing nowadays?
ZACK: I'm with the waterworks.
JACK: Oh, I see. Well, drop in some day.

SON: Dad, what is a weapon?
DAD: Why, son, that's something that you fight with.
SON: Is Mama your weapon?

GENERAL CUSTER: I hear your name is Sitting Bull.
SITTING BULL: Yes.
GENERAL CUSTER: Then why aren't you sitting?
SITTING BULL: I'm on vacation.

LESLIE: What do you take when you are run down?
LOUIS: Vitamins?
LESLIE: No. The license number.

HE: Isn't it wonderful how little chicks get out of their shells?
SHE: It's more wonderful how they get in.

The boy announced that he was going to feed his sheep ironized yeast. His father asked him why.

He said, "So I'll be able to get steel wool."

LORA: What do you do for a living?
GRANT: I'm a psychoanalyst in a candy factory.
LORA: What do you do there?
GRANT: I grade the nuts.

FIRST FARMER: Potato bugs ate my crop in ten days.
SECOND FARMER: They ate mine in three days, then roosted in the trees to see if I would plant some more.
SEED MERCHANT: That's nothing. Look there. Now there's one on my desk going through my books to see who ordered seed for next spring.

MAN: What are you looking for, son?
BOY: My watch.
MAN: Where did you lose it?
BOY: Up the street a ways.
MAN: Why are you looking for it here?
BOY: It was running when I dropped it.

HUSBAND: The laundry made a mistake and sent me the wrong shirt. The collar is so tight I can hardly breathe.

WIFE: That's your shirt alright, but you've got your head through the buttonhole.

WANDA: Why are you doing your painting all bundled up like that?
JACK: Well, it says right here on the paint can to be sure to put on three coats.

A native of Niagara Falls was showing the falls to a Texan.
NATIVE: I'll bet you don't have anything like that in Texas.
TEXAN: No, I reckon we don't, but we got plumbers that could fix it.

MOTHER: Tommy, did you fall down with your good pants on?
TOMMY: Yes, Mother, there wasn't time to take them off.

DRIVING INSTRUCTOR: Now, tell me. What would you do if your brakes suddenly failed to work?
STUDENT: I'd try to hit something cheap.

TED: I'm stronger than Tarzan.
FRED: No, you're not.
TED: Yes, I am.
FRED: How?
TED: I can beat my chest without hollering.

FIRST BURGLAR: How do you get away from the bloodhounds?
SECOND BURGLAR: I throw a penny in the river, and they follow the wrong cent.

PHYLLIS: Why wasn't the moon out last night?
CONNIE: Oh. Haven't you heard? They sent a mouse up in a rocket and it ate all the green cheese.

There were three men in a boat halfway across a lake. The first man suddenly said, "I forgot my lunch," got out of the boat, and walked to shore on top of the water.
Later, the second man said, "I forgot my fishing tackle," and also walked across the water to shore.
By this time, the third man thought to himself, "They're not going to outsmart me; I forgot my bait can," and he started to walk across the water, but he sank.
The first man turned to the second man and asked, "Do you think we should have told him where the rocks are?"

MOTHER: Eat your spinach, dear. It will put color in your cheeks.
LITTLE GIRL: Who wants green cheeks?

One day a very nervous lady was introduced to a prominent astronomer.

"Do you think that it's possible for the atom bomb to destroy the earth?" was her first question.

"Suppose it does," replied the great scientist casually. "After all, it isn't as if the earth were a major planet."

WILMA: Why isn't Beatle Bubble Bath Powder any good?
PAUL: I don't know. Why?
WILMA: It leaves a Ringo around your bathtub.

WANDA: Your pants look rather sad today.
NICK: What do you mean?
WANDA: *De*pressed.

MOTHER: Stop asking so many questions. Don't you know that curiosity killed the cat?
LESLIE: Really? What did the cat want to know?

Benjamin Franklin may have discovered electricity, but the man who invented the meter made all the money.

JOYCE: Dad, what should I wear with my green and purple socks?
DAD: Hip boots.

PILOT (who has just landed in a tree): I was trying to make a new record.
FARMER: You did. You're the first man ever to climb down that tree before he climbed up.

NATE: Can you let me have five dollars for a month, old boy?
ERIC: What would a month-old boy want with five dollars?

Did you hear about the man who fell into the lens-grinding machine and made a spectacle of himself?

A man was walking along the beach during high tide and decided that he wanted a bucket of salt water. A lifeguard jokingly charged him twenty-five cents. The man, returning at low tide, said to the lifeguard, "Boy, you sure had good business today."

SARAH: I took the recipe for this cake out of the cookbook.
RICK: Good. It never should have been there in the first place.

HUSBAND: Good news. I've saved enough money so that we can go to Europe this summer.
WIFE: Wonderful. When are we leaving?

HUSBAND: As soon as I've saved enough money for us to come back.

JANICE: I made two kinds of biscuits today. Would you like to take your pick?
TOM: No. I'd better use a hammer.

Two old ladies got on a plane. One went up to the pilot and said: "Sonny, please don't go faster than the speed of sound. My friend and I want to talk all the way."

TONY: I found a horseshoe today. What does it mean?
SALLY: Some poor horse is running around in his stocking feet.

A mathematics professor complained to a policeman that a driver had almost run him down as he had been trying to cross the street.
"Did you get his license number?" asked the policeman.
"Well, not exactly," the professor said. "But I do remember noticing that if it were doubled and then multiplied by itself, the square root of the product would be the original number with the integers reversed."

A father took his young son to the opera for the first time. The conductor started waving the baton, and the soprano began her aria. The boy watched everything intently and finally asked: "Why is he hitting her with his stick?"

"He's not hitting her," said the father with a chuckle.

"Well, then," asked the boy, "why is she screaming?"

INJURED PEDESTRIAN: What's the matter with you? Are you blind?
DRIVER: What do you mean, blind? I hit you, didn't I?

FLYING INSTRUCTOR: Fifty per cent of the people down there thought that we would be killed that time.
STUDENT: Yes, and fifty per cent of those up here thought so too.

JIM: Do you know why you can't write to Washington?
GARY: No, why?
JIM: Because he's dead. But you can still write to Lincoln.
GARY: But he's dead, too.
JIM: But he left his Gettysburg address.

STEVE: Do you know how I keep my head above water?
JULIE: Sure. Wood floats.

MR. KANE: Have any of your childhood wishes ever come true?

MR. PANE: Yes, one. When my brother used to pull my hair, I wished I didn't have any.

SUSAN: What job did you hold in the Army?
RALPH: Camp optometrist.
SUSAN: What did you do?
RALPH: My job was to cut eyes out of potatoes.

The lady's car stalled at a traffic light. She couldn't get it started again. The driver of the car behind her automobile honked and honked and honked. Finally, she got out of her car, walked up to the impatient driver, and said, "There is something wrong with my car. Maybe you can get out and help. I'll sit in your car and blow your horn for you."

A boy gave his girl friend a corsage with a note saying, "With all my love and most of my allowance."

DARLENE: Why are you writing so fast?
FRED: So I can finish before my pen runs out of ink.

SON: I went out for the football team.
FATHER: Did you make it?
SON: Well, I think I did. The coach looked at me and said, "This is the end."

SON: Dad, Mom was backing out of the garage and she ran over my bike.
FATHER: Well, it serves you right. How many times have I told you not to leave your bike on the porch?

MOTHER: Why is my picture in little pieces?
JERRY: Well, you told the man to have it blown up.

Isn't it strange that no matter where you sit at a ball game, you're always located right between the hot dog peddler and his best customer?

JERRY: I fell over twenty feet last night.
JUDY: Were you hurt?
JERRY: No. I was just trying to get to my seat in a movie theater.

VERNON: When I grow up, everybody will look up to me.
VERONICA: How's that?
VERNON: I'm going to be a window washer.

FIRST AID INSTRUCTOR: What would you do in the case of a man bleeding from a wound in the head?
STUDENT: Put a tourniquet around his neck.

HE: There is a new invention that I think is marvelous. It shines a beam of invisible light two hundred feet into a mirror which reflects the shaft back into an electronic tube. The whole device is installed on the rooftop of a high building in a big city. When the smog gets really bad, the sensitive tube rings a bell.
SHE: So?
HE: Don't you see? Now you not only see and smell smog, you can hear it.

CHILD: And what did you do when your ship sank?
OLD CAPTAIN: Oh, I grabbed a cake of soap and washed myself ashore.

MARK: Why are you wearing your socks inside out?
STEVE: My feet got hot, so I turned the hose on them.

"Pilot to control tower! Pilot to control tower! I'm coming in. Please give me landing instructions."

"Control tower to pilot. Control tower to pilot. Why are you yelling so loud?"
"Pilot to control tower! Pilot to control tower! I don't have a radio."

SAILOR: This boat makes fifteen knots an hour.
LITTLE GIRL: Who unties them?

LINDA: My father drives a stagecoach without wheels.
CINDY: What holds it up?
LINDA: Bandits.

JACK: Mom, I'm going out to play.
MOTHER: With those holes in your socks?
JACK: No. With the boy across the street.

KATHY: Did you hear about the man that protested his job by eating?
HAL: No.
KATHY: He was all fed up with it.

A baby sardine was swimming happily when he saw his first submarine. Badly frightened, he swam over to his mother's side. "Don't worry," she assured him. "It's just a can of people."

PAT: Plug in the clock.
PAM: OK.

PAT: Is it running?
PAM: No.
PAT: How come?
PAM: Because it has no legs.

WRESTLING COACH: What can our wrestling team's colors be?
WRESTLER: How about black and blue?

A little boy said to his father after listening to him read a bedtime story: "OK, so the cow jumped over the moon. What about her re-entry into the earth's atmosphere?"

TERRY: Is your new home warm?
PERRY: It should be. The painter gave it two coats last month.

JAKE: My dog Tiger ran away.
MIKE: Why don't you put an ad in the paper?
JAKE: Tiger can't read.

GEORGE: When they take your appendix out, it's called an appendectomy; when they remove your tonsils from your throat, it's called a tonsillectomy. What is it when you remove a growth from your head?
STAN: I give up.
GEORGE: A haircut.

CARL: Tom, look out for the worms in that apple.

TOM: When I eat apples, the worms better look out for themselves.

MOTHER: Have you given the goldfish fresh water today?

DAUGHTER: No. They haven't finished the water I gave them yesterday.

A man from Texas and a man from Connecticut were talking. The man from Texas said, "You can get on a train in Texas and the next day you will still be in Texas."

"Well," said the man from Connecticut, "we're used to slow trains in Connecticut, too."

A seasoned paratrooper, home on furlough, took a regular commercial flight from San Francisco eastward. As the plane prepared to land in Chicago, the paratrooper nervously peered out of the window and adjusted his safety belt several times.

Noticing this, the flight attendant asked, "You seem nervous. Haven't you ever been up in a plane before?"

"Sure," stammered the paratrooper. "I've been up in planes dozens of times, but this is the first time I've ever come down in one."

AUNT: Marlene certainly has her mother's eyes.
GRANDMOTHER: And her father's nose.
SISTER: And my new dress.

MONICA: If the astronauts landed back on earth on land instead of water, what would you call it?
GREG: Smashdown.

CAROL: Why did the orange stop in the middle of the road?
JEAN: It ran out of juice.

LONNIE: Mother, may I please have half-a-dollar for the man who is crying outside the house?
MOTHER: What's he crying about?
LONNNIE: He's crying, "Ice cream sticks—fifty cents."

ONE GOSSIP TO ANOTHER: It's so annoying. She told me not to tell anyone, and everyone I tell has already heard it.

GRANDMOTHER: Go wash your face, Lucy dear. I can see what you had for breakfast this morning.
LUCY: What was it?
GRANDMOTHER: Eggs.
LUCY: You're wrong. I had eggs yesterday.

LAURA: I hear that they are making the Leaning Tower of Pisa into a hotel.
MAX: Really? What are they going to call it?
LAURA: The Tiltin' Hilton.

MOTHER: What do you want to take your cod-liver oil with?
DAUGHTER: With a fork.

MOTHER: Sometimes your father takes things apart to see why they don't work.
DENNIS: So what?
MOTHER: So you had better work.

A man was introduced to a circus sword swallower. Not having seen a sword swallower before, the man asked him to demonstrate his act. So the fellow ate some pins and needles.
"But," said the man, "those aren't swords."
"I know," was the reply. "I'm on a diet."

A football coach with a reputation for optimism came into the locker room to give his boys a pre-game pep talk. "Alright, boys," he cried cheerfully. "Here we are—unbeaten, untied, and unscored-on—and ready for the first game of the season."

CATHY: Did you hear about the glassblower who inhaled?

KARL: No. What happened?
CATHY: Now he has a pane in his side.

SON: A train just passed.
DAD: How do you know?
SON: I saw its tracks.

Two ladies had each just bought a Volkswagen Beetle. One of the ladies was standing by her car with the hood up. The other lady drove by and asked her what was wrong.

"Somebody stole the engine out of my car," she said.

"Oh, don't worry about it," her friend said. "I just found out that I have a spare engine in my trunk and I'll be glad to lend it to you."

BARBARA: I'll always have a soft spot in my heart for you.
BOB: Then let's get married.
BARBARA: I said a soft spot in my heart, not in my head.

JOANNA: Ouch! That water is so hot it burned my hand.
BRUCE: Serves you right. You should have felt it before you put your hand in it.

PASSENGER: Do I take this train to Washington?
CONDUCTOR: No. The engineer will do that.

DONNA: I can tell you what the score of the game will be before it starts.
DORIS: What?
DONNA: Nothing to nothing.

ROLAND: Have you forgotten that you owe me five dollars?
HAROLD: No. Not yet. Give me time and I will.

HELEN: I know a man who ran over himself.
GWEN: How did he do that?
HELEN: Well, he asked me to run across the street to mail a letter.
GWEN: What did you say?
HELEN: I said, "No," so he ran over himself.

NORMAN: I dreamed last night that I had invented a new type of breakfast food. I was sampling it when . . .
ANN: Yes, yes. Go on.
NORMAN: I woke up and found a corner of my mattress gone.

CLIFF: What would you do if a man-eating tiger chased you?
DIANE: Nothing. I'm a girl.

INSPECTOR FROM THE BUREAU OF WEIGHTS AND MEASURES TO BUTCHER: We've had some complaints that you have devalued the pound.

ANDREW: Hey, Rachel, did you see the moon last night?
RACHEL: What channel?

BILL: How did you break your arm?
BOB: You see those steps over there?
BILL: Yes.
BOB: Well, I didn't.

ONE GOSSIP to ANOTHER: I won't go into details. I've told you more about it than I heard myself.

GREG: I saw you running to school alongside your bike this morning.
STELLA: Yes. I was very late and I didn't have time to get on.

ALEX: Does your cow give milk?
FARMER: Not exactly. You sorta have to take it away from her.

KAREN: Your sister is spoiled, isn't she?
DORIS: No. That's just the perfume she is wearing.

PASSENGER: Which end of the car do I get off?
CONDUCTOR: Either one. It stops at both ends.

MARILYN: There is one good thing about smog.
MORTY: What is that?

MARILYN: You can at least see what you are breathing.

After seeing a jet plane fly past, the male bird said to his mate, "I'll bet I could fly that fast, too, if my tail were on fire."

ANITA: A crab just bit off my toe.
ARNOLD: Which one?
ANITA: I don't know. All crabs look alike to me.

BOB: Where do you keep your six goldfish?
ELSIE: In the bathtub.
BOB: What do you do with them when you take a bath?
ELSIE: I blindfold them.

MAN (coming back and finding a stranger sitting in his chair): You're sitting in my chair.
STRANGER: Can you prove it?
MAN: I think I left my cake and ice cream on it.

Did you hear about the farmer who figured out a way to water his potatoes? He planted them with the onions, so that the onions would make the potatoes' eyes water.

SPYROS: What happened to the members of the Invisible Men's Club?

LANA: Can't find out. Nobody has seen them lately.

CRANDALL: I haven't slept for ten days.
LISA: Aren't you tired?
CRANDALL: No. I sleep nights.

LOLA: I have a car that has no engine and no wheels. All it has is a horn.
PAUL: How does it go?
LOLA: BEEP! BEEP!

WIFE: Don't forget to bring home another mousetrap.
HUSBAND: What's the matter with the one I bought yesterday?
WIFE: It's full.

CALVIN: Television will never take the place of the newspaper.
IRVING: Why not?
CALVIN: Have you ever tried to swat a fly with a TV set?

SCOUTMASTER: How do you make a bedroll?
TENDERFOOT: Push it.

A minister of a small church was awakened one night by a suspicious noise. Out of the darkness came a voice: "Don't move or I'll shoot. I'm looking for your money."

"Let me get up and turn on the light," begged the minister. "I'll hunt, too."

MRS. HICKS: Did you meet your son at the store?
MRS. SNEED: Oh, my goodness, no. I've known him for years.

COUNSELOR: How can you do so many silly things in one day?
CAMPER: I get up early.

A baseball batter hit a foul ball and it landed on the umpire's head. The umpire began to walk all over the field. He finally fell down. One of the spectators yelled out: "You have just witnessed the fall of the roamin' umpire."

TWO-YEAR-OLD (watching his father change a flat tire): Daddy, what are you doing?
FATHER: Changing a tire.
TWO-YEAR-OLD: Why? Is it wet?

ANN: Did you hear about the angel who lost his job?
ANDY: No. What happened?
ANN: He had harp failure.

FARM VISITOR: Is Ballpoint really the name of your pig?
FARMER: No. That's just his pen name.

A six-year-old girl came rushing home from school filled with news about her new boyfriend. "He's so smart," she said. "He just knows all about first grade."
"How's that?" her mother asked.
The little girl replied, "Oh, he was there last year."

MARGOT: I didn't sleep well last night.
MIKE: Why not?
MARGOT: By mistake, I plugged the electric blanket into the toaster and I kept popping out of bed all night.

FATHER: Son, you're studying accounting now, aren't you?
SON: Yes, Dad.
FATHER: Then start accounting for why the car wasn't in the garage last night.

SHE: It must be difficult for a man with a moustache to eat soup.
HE: Yes. Quite a strain.

SYLVIA: How did you like your first ride on a horse?

ELWOOD: I didn't know that anything filled with hay could be so hard.

HUSBAND: Aren't you ready yet?
WIFE: I told you an hour ago that I would be ready in a few minutes.

Did you know that a needle is the only thing that can work with something in its eye?

BRENDA: I'll bet you a quarter that I've got the hardest name in the world.
ANN: Alright. What's your name?
BRENDA: Stone.
ANN: Pay me the quarter. My name is Harder.

A candidate out canvassing for votes knocked at a door. When a lady opened the door, he said, "Are you on the electoral register of this constituency?"
"Sorry," she replied. "We cook with gas."

Watch out for the guy who comes up and slaps you on the back. He's bound to expect you to cough up something.

WAITRESS: Don't I know you from somewhere?
FAMOUS ACTOR: You may have seen me in the movies.
WAITRESS: Maybe. Where do you usually sit?

HUSBAND: Where in heaven's name does all that grocery money go that I give you?
WIFE: Stand aside and look in the mirror.

LADY: What is your cat's name, little boy?
BOY: Ben Hur.
LADY: That's a strange name for a cat. How did you happen to choose that?
BOY: Well, we just called him Ben until he had kittens.

The little boy came into the room where his parents were sitting and said, "Did you hear the weather predicament on the radio?"
"Oh, isn't that cute?" the mother said to the boy's father.
"That's prediction, not predicament," corrected the father.
"Oh no," said the little boy, "the guy on the radio said we're getting a hurricane, and that's a predicament."

STAN: Gosh, I'm downhearted.
GARY: But why should you be if your girl said that she would be faithful to the end?
STAN: Because I'm the halfback.

GIRL: I'm not myself tonight.
BOY: Then we ought to have a good time.

MOTHER: Why is your brother crying?
BOY: Because I won't give him my piece of cake.
MOTHER: Is his piece gone?
BOY: Yes. He cried when I ate that piece, too.

BOSS: Any messages for me while I was out?
SECRETARY: Yes, sir. One of the ducks you were hunting last weekend called and left her number.

FATHER: What happened to that waterproof, shockproof, unbreakable, antimagnetic watch that we gave you for Christmas last year, son?
SON: I lost it.

MOTHER: Did you mail my letter? It was an important one, you know.
TIM: Yes, ma'am. Indeed I did.
MOTHER: But why have you brought back the fifteen cents that I gave you to buy the stamp?
TIM: I didn't have to use it. I put the letter in the mailbox when no one was looking.

SUSAN: Will you change a dime for me?
TAD: Of course.
SUSAN: Then change it into a quarter.

MR. AXELROD: My fifteen-year-old son is an excellent piano player. He can even play with his feet.

MR. PRATHER: That's nothing. My son can play with his feet and he's only one year old.

NATURE GUIDE: Now let's talk about the bear. Do we get fur from him?

CAMPER: Myself, I'd get as fur from him as possible.

SON: Dad, have you noticed what's new in boys' clothes this year?

FATHER: Yes, son. Girls.

Then there was the karate expert who stuck his hand out for a left turn and smashed up a Volkswagen.

AARON: I don't know whether to get a job in a barber shop or spend my life writing novels.

TOM: Toss a coin. Heads or tales.

MOTHER TIGER: Junior, what are you doing?

JUNIOR: I'm chasing a hunter around the tree.

MOTHER TIGER: Stop that! How many times have I told you not to play with your food?

LINDA: If a man smashed a clock, would he be accused of killing time?

MINDY: Not if the clock struck first.

Two ladies met on the street. "Oh, Grace," said one. "So many things have happened since I saw you last. I've had all my teeth removed, and a new stove and refrigerator put in."

MAX: Dad, I think I need glasses.
DAD: Why, son?
MAX: I can't see in the dark.

Because of a dense fog, a Mississippi steamboat had to stop at the mouth of a river. A woman passenger demanded to know the cause of the delay.

"Can't see up the river," the harassed captain said. "Fog's too thick."

"But I can see the stars overhead," the woman replied.

"Yes," the captain said. "But unless the boilers explode, we aren't going that way."

NEAL: Did you know that Michelangelo spent seven years painting the ceiling of the Sistine Chapel in Rome and then got mad at the monks?
LIVIA: Why did he get mad?
NEAL: They asked for a second coat.

MARK: For my science project I invented something that will allow people to see through walls.

JILL: Gee, that's great. What are you going to call it?

MARK: A window.

LEAH: How do you like my paint colors?

HOLLIS: I wish I could take them home with me.

LEAH: You can. You just sat on them.

DAN: I get up when the first ray of sunshine strikes my window.

JAN: Isn't that rather early?

DAN: No. My room faces west.

ANGIE: Who is Richard Stans?

BERYL: I don't know.

ANGIE: He must be pretty important, because each morning in school we say, "I pledge allegiance to the flag of the United States of America and to the Republic of Richard Stans."

WIFE: Anything new in the paper, dear?

HUSBAND: Yes. There's been an earthquake in a town called Drakgslievwykstik.

WIFE: Does it say what the town was called before the earthquake?

SANFORD: Did you know that the animals in Noah's ark came in pairs?

GRACE: Yes. All except the worms. They came in apples.

CARLOTTA: I wish I had been born in the Dark Ages.
KATE: So do I. You look terrible in the light.

A very fat man and a very thin man collided on the street.
FAT MAN: From the looks of you, there's been a famine around here.
THIN MAN: From the looks of you, you caused it.

DENISE: What are you looking for?
RICK: A girl.
DENISE: Here I am.
RICK: Good. You can help me look.

An American tourist was in his bathing suit in the middle of the desert. An Arab rode up to him and blinked in amazement.
TOURIST: I'm going swimming in the ocean.
ARAB: But the ocean is eight hundred miles from here.
TOURIST: Eight hundred miles? Boy, what a beach.

GREG: Did you know that they found little bugs in the moon soil?

PAUL: No. What were they?
GREG: Luna-ticks.

DOUG: How many letters are there in the alphabet?
LIL: Twenty-six.
DOUG: No. Twenty-one. L&M just got kicked out for smoking and TWA just took off.

FATHER: At your age I could name all of the Presidents in the proper order.
SON: Yes, but there were only three or four of them then.

LYNN: You have your shoes on the wrong feet.
WINTHROP: How could I? These are the only feet I have.

There is an old adage: "Man who sits on hot stove soon rises in the world."

MESS SERGEANT: Look here, Private, I was cooking chow long before you were born.
PRIVATE: OK, but why serve it now?

FIRST AID INSTRUCTOR: When a baby swallows a coin, what should you do?
STUDENT: Call the tax collector. He can get money out of anyone.

MARCIA: My sister is a magician. She can turn into a rabbit.

JOHN: That's nothing. I can walk to the corner and turn into a drugstore.

FIRST COWBOY: Why do you wear only one spur?

SECOND COWBOY: Well, I figure when one side of the horse starts running, the other side will, too.

ELSIE: How did you get a ticket to the circus?
DON: It's my brother's ticket.
ELSIE: Where is your brother?
DON: Home looking for his ticket.

POLLY: I was told that your wife is a finished soprano.

SAM: No, not yet, but the neighbors nearly got her last night.

FATHER: Your new brother has just arrived.
CHILD: Where did he come from?
FATHER: From a faraway country.
CHILD: What? Another alien?

FATHER: Son, I think it is time that we talked about the facts of life.
SON: Sure, Dad. What do you want to know?

POSTMAN: Does this package belong to you? The name is obliterated.
MR. ALLEN: Can't be mine then. My name is Allen.

STRANGER: How old is your little baby sister?
LITTLE BROTHER: She's this year's model.

VIRGIL: Look at that horse there standing on three legs, scratching his stomach with his hind hoof. I wonder what's the matter with him.
GRACE: Nothing is wrong with him. He's just feeling his oats.

It used to be that Father dealt out the discipline to Junior. Then the safety razor took away his razor strop, furnaces took away his woodshed, and baldness took away his hairbrush. That's why kids are running wild today. Fathers ran out of weapons.

Rick was up on a ladder helping to paint Tom's house. From the ground, Tom asked, "Have you got a good grip on your brush, Rick?"
"You bet," answered Rick.
"Make sure," said Tom. "I'm going to move the ladder."

FATHER: Have you been reading those horse stories again?
DAUGHTER: Yes, Father.
FATHER: That's why you have so many nightmares.

RALPH: Norman, do you have a half brother?
NORMAN: No. They come in one piece.

SAL: I can lie in my bed and watch the sun rise.
MARGO: So what? I can stand in our living room and watch the kitchen sink.

DEREK (at a birthday party): That's the fourth time you have gone back for ice cream and cake. Doesn't it embarrass you?
WARREN: Why should it? I tell the hostess that it's for you.

MARY: My room is decorated in the Early French style.
GARY: Mine is done in Japanese Modern.
LARRY: Well, mine is in contemporary disorder.

LOST BALLOONIST: Ahoy below. Where am I?
STARTLED FARMER: Heh, heh. You can't fool me. You're up there in that little basket.

KIRSTIN: This is an ideal spot for a picnic.
RAMONA: It must be. Fifty million insects can't be wrong.

MOTHER: Where have you been? The FBI was looking for you.
SON: The FBI?
MOTHER: Yes. Father, Brother, and I.

SERAFINA: Isn't it fantastic? Just think, light from the sun travels at a rate of one hundred eighty-six thousand miles a second.
JEFF: Big deal! It's downhill all the way.

TEACHER: LeRoy, this homework looks like it is in your father's handwriting.
LEROY: Sure. I used his fountain pen.

TIM: Is your new hunting horse well behaved?
BART: Yes. When we come to a fence, he stops and lets me over first.

A man wanted to be a postman and had to take an examination. The first question was: "How far is it to the moon?"
The man answered it: "If the moon is going to be on my route, I won't accept the job."

Little Enos, who had never seen a dish of Jell-O, sat at the dinner table staring at it for a long time, watching it quiver. "Go ahead and eat it," his mother said.

"Eat it?" The boy drew back in amazement. "I can't. It isn't dead yet."

HELMUT: Do you know why a mother kangaroo hates rain?
DAISY: No. Why?
HELMUT: Because the children have to play inside.

A tobacco farmer was showing a visiting lady around his plantation.
FARMER: These are tobacco plants in full bloom.
LADY: Isn't that wonderful. When will the cigars be ripe?

MOTHER: Ronnie, there were two pieces of pie in the kitchen this morning, and now there is only one. How is that?
RONNIE: I don't know. It was so dark this morning I guess I didn't see the other piece.

KAREN: My cat is smart.
CARL: How come?
KAREN: Because it eats cheese and then stands by the rat hole, with baited breath.

SON: Mom, what was the name of the last station where our train stopped?

MOTHER: I don't know. And don't bother me. Can't you see I'm reading?

SON: Well, it's too bad that you don't know, because little brother got off there.

Tom and Bill were fishing one day. They were catching a lot of fish in one spot and they wanted to mark the spot. "I'll mark the bottom of the boat with a piece of chalk," said Tom.

"You are so stupid," said Bill. "What happens if we don't get the same boat tomorrow?"

The paratroopers were aloft for their first jump. Everything went off in perfect order until the last man came forward to jump.

"Hold it!" shouted his commanding officer. "You're not wearing your parachute."

"Oh, that's alright, sir," said the recruit. "We're just practicing, aren't we?"

MELINDA: Do you have a brother?

JACK: No, but the funny thing is that my sister has one.

LAURIE: Do you know that they are now making frozen Band-Aids?

KIM: Really? What for?

LAURIE: For cold cuts.

FATHER: You're staying up too late, son.
SON: I know, Dad. I'm doing my homework.
FATHER: How do you expect to get up in the morning?
SON: Slo-o-o-owly.

A mother kangaroo took her baby out of her pouch, spanked her soundly, and said, "Don't you ever eat crackers in bed again."

DAFFY: Why does your dog keep turning around in circles?
RANDY: He's a watchdog and he's winding himself up.

FRANK: Why are you shivering?
GWEN: It's the falling stars.
FRANK: Why, falling stars can't hurt you.
GWEN: It's not the stars I'm worried about. It's whoever is throwing them.

CARMEN: I don't like to repeat gossip, but . . .
JOANNE: But what else can you do with it?

BOB: I was on television today.
DAVID: For how long?
BOB: Until my mother came into the living room and told me to jump down.

An atomic scientist went on vacation. In his absence, a sign was hung on his office door reading: "Gone fission."

BOY: Since I met you, I can't eat, I can't sleep, and I can't go out with my friends.
GIRL: Why not?
BOY: I'm broke.

A widow married several years after her first husband died. After the ceremony, her oldest son started passing out cigars.
"It's a Dad," he said.

The older sister, who was entertaining her boyfriend at dinner, spoke to her younger sister, who had set the table: "Why didn't you put a knife and fork at Joe's place?"
The younger sister answered, "I didn't think he needed them. You said he eats like a horse."

According to unofficial sources, a new, simplified income tax form for next year contains only four lines:
1. What was your income last year?
2. What were your expenses?
3. How much have you left?
4. Send it in.

"I've got to find the candy I dropped," said a man searching under the table.

"Never mind, dear," said his wife. "Take another one."

"I've got to find that one," her husband replied. "My teeth are in it."

QUENTIN: I used to race cars.
ANDY: Why did you quit?
QUENTIN: I couldn't run fast enough.

Then there was the wife who was an old hand at acupuncture—she kept needling her husband.

SON: Dad, what does transatlantic mean?
FATHER: It means across the Atlantic.
SON: Does trans always mean across?
FATHER: Yes.
SON: Then transparent means a cross father.

SLAVE DRIVER: Listen, galley slaves. I have some good news and some bad news for you. First, the good news. Everyone will get an extra ration of food for lunch.
SLAVES: Hurray!
SLAVE DRIVER: Now for the bad news. After lunch, the captain wants to go water skiing.

CAPTAIN: What are you scratching your head for, Private Honeywell?
HONEYWELL: I guess I've got arithmetic bugs.
CAPTAIN: What are arithmetic bugs?
HONEYWELL: Fleas.

CAPTAIN: Why do you call them arithmetic bugs?

HONEYWELL: Because they add to my misery, subtract from my pleasure, divide my attention, and multiply like the dickens.

YOUNG HEN: How do you manage to stay around so long?
OLD HEN: Well, I follow a good rule.
YOUNG HEN: What's that?
OLD HEN: An egg a day keeps the axe away.

Television newscaster reading note: "A late bulletin just handed to me: 'You've got a piece of spinach or something between your two top teeth.'"

FIRST WORKER: Hey, did you hear about the fellow who got hurt today?
SECOND WORKER: No. What happened?
FIRST WORKER: He got run over by a steamroller. He's in the hospital in rooms thirty-one to thirty-five.

GABE: Mom, I just knocked down the ladder that was standing up against the side of the house.
MOTHER: Go tell your father.
GABE: He already knows. He's hanging on to the roof.

DR. KANGEROO: What seems to be the matter, Mrs. Kangaroo?
MRS. KANGAROO: I don't know. I haven't been feeling jumpy lately.

BARBARA: We passed your house today.
LUCILLE: Thanks. We appreciate it.

HUGO: Why are you digging a hole?
KERMIT: I feel low down.

LES: Did you get hurt when you were on the football team?
BUTCH: Nope. It was just while the whole team was on me.

DON: Are those your dogs?
MARIE: Yes, they are.
DON: What are their names?
MARIE: George and Henry.
DON: Which one is George?
MARIE: The one standing beside Henry.

FATHER (on Memorial Day): Where is Mother, Ted?
TED: Upstairs, waving her hair.
FATHER: Can't we afford a flag?

SINGER: Do you like my voice?
ACCOMPANIST: Madam, I've played on the

white keys, and I've played on the black keys, but you are the first person I've heard who sings in the cracks.

   ROCK: Did you see the cute chick going down the road, Burt?
   BURT: No, I didn't. What did she look like?
   ROCK: She was about three and a half inches high, had two legs and feathers, and was walking behind the mother hen.

   GERT: Have you ever had your eyes checked?
   SANDY: No, they've always been blue.

   CLEO: Is your toaster a pop-up?
   FRAN: No. It's an Indian model.
   CLEO: How come?
   FRAN: It sends up smoke signals.

   Triumphant father to mother watching teen-age son shoveling the sidewalk: "I told him I lost the car keys in the snow."

   SUSIE: I'm on my way to get some sealing wax.
   CYNTHIA: Why would you want to wax the ceiling?

   "My wife gets after me for my use of the English language. I can speak as well as she can—as a matter of fact, weller."

TEACHER: Come up here and give me what you have in your mouth.
STUDENT: I wish I could. It's a sore tooth.

HE: What is big at the bottom, little at the top, and has ears?
SHE: I don't know.
HE: A mountain.
SHE: But what about the ears?
HE: Haven't you heard about mountaineers?

WIFE: Do you feel like a cup of coffee?
HUSBAND: Why, no. Do I look like one?

MOTHER: James, how did this window get broken?
JAMES: I was cleaning my slingshot and it went off.

RITA: Harvey, are you using your lawn mower this afternoon?
HARVEY: Yes, I'm afraid I am.
RITA: Then you won't be using your tennis racket. I've broken mine.

KAREN: Did you know that you will never again see a full moon?
ARNIE: How come?
KAREN: The astronauts brought part of it back with them.

The principal of a school wouldn't let the star football player play in the big game. The coach brought the player into the principal's office and cried: "Why won't you let him play? We need him."

"I'll tell you why," snapped the principal. "This is supposed to be a place of learning. All he knows is football. I'll show you how much he knows." Then he asked the player, "How much is two plus two?"

"Seven," came the answer.

The coach argued, "Aw, let him play. He only missed it by one."

It will be a while before cars will be pollution-free. For the moment, that's emission impossible.

CARPENTER: Didn't I tell you to notice when the glue boiled over?
ASSISTANT: I did. It was a quarter past ten.

A passerby saw a man struggling with a piano in a doorway. He offered his help, which was gladly accepted. Both tugged and pulled for an hour until the owner of the piano gasped, "At this rate it will take us hours to get it out."

"Out?" screamed the other man. "Why didn't you say you wanted it out? I've been trying to push it in."

MILLIONAIRE: I want to make a plane reservation for a trip around the world.
TRAVEL CLERK: Yes, sir. One way?

HAROLD: Dad, is it true that the law of gravity keeps us on our planet?
FATHER: Yes.
HAROLD: What did we do before the law was passed?

SHELLY: I'm going to open up a pet shop. When you see me next, I'll be among the little dumb animals.
GASTON: Wear a hat so I will recognize you.

HE: What's a confirmed loser?
SHE: One who puts his ear to a seashell and gets a busy signal.

LITTLE BOY: Daddy, Daddy, I only had one cavity.
FATHER: Great!
PASSERBY: How did he do it?
FATHER: He only has two teeth.

GRETCHEN: Have you heard of the new soap?
RUDY: What's it called?
GRETCHEN: It's called Lumpo. Lumpo doesn't clean, doesn't lather, doesn't bubble.
RUDY: What does it do?

GRETCHEN: It just lies there on the bottom of the tub and keeps you company.

CHRIS: Did you know that an apple a day will keep the doctor away?
JAMES: Yes, but did you know that an onion a day will keep everybody away?

LARRY: Sue, I hear that you have a new baby sister. What's her name?
SUE: I don't know. She won't tell me.

THEATER USHER: How far down do you want to sit, madam?
THEATER PATRON: Why, all the way down, of course.

A famous editor was traveling in unexplored country and was captured by cannibals. He was put in the pot to boil and from the way he carried on it was obvious he was not very happy about the situation. The chief of the cannibals saw how upset he was and decided to talk to him.

"My good man," said the chief to the editor, "I wouldn't be so distressed. Why, in only a short time you will be an editor-in-chief."

CHARLEY: My friend Socko the boxer had four straight knock-outs and then he retired.

CRANDALL: Why did he retire?
CHARLEY: He got tired of being knocked out.

TONY: Once I was a ninety-pound weakling. One day, on the beach, a two-hundred-pound bully kicked sand in my face. So I exercised hard every day, and now I'm two hundred pounds and strong, so I went to the beach.
CHERYL: What happened?
TONY: A four-hundred-pound bully kicked sand in my face.

LADY: Why are you running around the block carrying that pack?
LITTLE BOY: I'm running away and I'm not allowed to cross the street.

CITY LADY (talking to ranch hand): Have you ever had any accidents?
RANCH HAND: Nah, but once a rattlesnake bit me and a horse kicked me.
CITY LADY: Oh, dear. Don't you call those accidents?
RANCH HAND: Of course not. Them critters did it on purpose.

BILL: Hey, Fred, do you know how to drive a chameleon crazy?

FRED: No. How?
BILL: Hold it up to your plaid shirt.

SCIENTIST: I've invented a way to make wool out of milk.
FRIEND: That's great, but doesn't it make the cow feel sheepish?

ROBBER: Here, take this money.
POOR MAN: Why?
ROBBER: Because I steal from the rich and give to the poor.
POOR MAN: Yippee! I'm rich.
ROBBER: OK. Stick 'em up.

EARL: My wife is very irritable. The least little thing starts her off.
DAN: You're lucky. Mine's a self-starter.

GIRL FRIEND: A little bird told me that you were going to buy me a ring.
BOYFRIEND: It must have been a cuckoo.

PAUL: I'm worried about my wife. She drives like lightning.
IAN: You mean she drives too fast?
PAUL: No, not that. She's always striking trees.

MOTHER: When that naughty boy threw stones at you, why didn't you come and tell me instead of throwing stones back at him?
BOY: What good would it have done to tell you? You couldn't hit the broad side of a barn.

A little boy was kneeling beside his bed, saying his prayers. His mother said, "I can't hear you."
The little boy answered, "I wasn't talking to you."

BIFF: It says here in the newspaper that a man is run over in New York every half hour.
HAL: The poor fellow.

WIFE (to husband): I always knew you had a photographic mind. Too bad it was never developed.

ZEKE: What is the darkest night you have ever seen?
LUKE: The darkest night I have ever seen was when the raindrops knocked at the door and asked for a light to see where to hit the ground.

MOE: Why is your eye black and blue?
JOE: I just got hit with tomatoes.

MOE: And you got those bad bruises from tomatoes?
JOE: The tomatoes were in the can.

The minister was confused at a wedding by the groom's long hair. He thought for a while, then smiled and said, "Will one of you please kiss the bride?"

A little boy got a shirt from his grandmother for his birthday. He wrote her a thank-you note:
"Dear Grandma: I liked the shirt you sent me for my birthday. I would like to write more, but I'm all choked up."

CAROL: Did you hear about the girl with the gleam in her eye?
JEAN: No.
CAROL: Her toothbrush slipped.

PHIL: Which team do you like the best, the White Sox or the Red Sox?
HANS: I prefer the Nylons.
PHIL: The Nylons? Never heard of them. What makes them so great?
HANS: They get more runs.

SARAH: Jim, did you hear what happened to the Idaho potato farmer's crop when he crossed a sponge with a potato?

JIM: No. What happened?
SARAH: They tasted horrible, but they sure soaked up a lot of gravy.

LATE-STAYING GUEST: I hope I haven't kept you up too late.
HOST: Not at all. We would have been getting up soon anyway.

GINA (at the movies): Oh my goodness! We must go right home.
MARK: What's wrong?
GINA: I forgot to turn off the iron. It might start a fire.
MARK: Don't worry. I forgot to turn off the water.

A boy was walking down the street pulling a rope. A man stopped him and asked, "Why are you pulling that rope?"
The boy said, "Well, have you ever tried to push one?"

JAKE: I see that your new telescope only magnifies ten times.
STAN: Oh, no. I've already used it twelve times.

BEVERLY: Did you cry at last night's movie?
TRISH: Yes. They wouldn't give me my money back.

RICK: Is your brother spoiled?
SHARON: No. He just needs a bath.

MAVIS: Did you hear the joke about the bed?
LOLA: No.
MAVIS: It hasn't been made up yet.

LITTLE BOY: Daddy, are bugs good to eat?
FATHER: Don't talk about it at the table, son.
FATHER (later): Now, what were you asking, son?
LITTLE BOY: There was a bug in your soup, but it's gone now.

A vacationing family loaded a pet squirrel, cage and all, into the front compartment of their foreign, rear-engine car. They stopped at a gas station and the father said, "Fill it up," and the family got out to look at the view.

When they came back, the father said, "How much do I owe you?"

The attendant said, "I don't know. I gave your engine two bags of peanuts, but I can't figure out how to test its oil."

HUSBAND: The doorbell doesn't work.
WIFE: What's the matter with it?
HUSBAND: It has a short circuit.
WIFE: Then lengthen it.

Two young girls were whispering in the movies and annoying a man sitting in front of them. Finally he turned around and said, "Girls, I can't hear a word."

One of the girls snapped at him: "Well, what we are discussing is none of your business."

TANYA: Why don't you answer the phone?
MARK: It isn't ringing.
TANYA: Why do you always have to wait until the last minute?

IGOR: I took a bath in milk last night.
GRETA: Was it pasteurized?
IGOR: No. It just came up to my knees.

OSCAR: My dog can talk.
RICK: What can he say?
OSCAR (to dog): Who was one of the greatest ballplayers of all time?
DOG: Roof! Roof!
OSCAR: That's right. Babe Roof.

GARDENER: Is this your baseball?
BOY: Are there any broken windows?
GARDENER: No.
BOY: Then it's mine.

JOHN: When you die, you ought to leave your head to science.

RON: Why?
JOHN: They're still trying to find the perfect vacuum.

ELLIOT: I want to go to the sun.
CAROL: You can't go to the sun, you'll burn up.
ELLIOT: No, I wouldn't. I'd go at night.

HUSBAND: You ought to run for Congress, dear.
WIFE: Why?
HUSBAND: Because you are so great at bringing bills into the house.

Did you hear of the absentminded professor who returned from lunch and saw a sign on his office door, "Back in thirty minutes," and sat down to wait for himself?

Did you hear of the absentminded professor who put out the clock and wound up the cat?

Did you hear of the absentminded professor who got up and struck a match to see if he had blown out the candle?

Here's an old saying: "A chemist who falls in a vat of acid is absorbed in his work."

MAILMAN: A dog bit my leg this morning.
BOSS: Did you put anything on it?
MAILMAN: No. He liked it just as it was.

PRIVATE: I think that every time the sergeant sees me he gets a headache.
CORPORAL: Why is that?
PRIVATE: Because when he sees me he yells, "Tension."

GRACE: I can pick up Mexico City on my radio.
GLENN: That's nothing. I can open my window and get Chile.

A group of students was protesting at a local factory that had been polluting a stream. One of the students was recognized as the daughter of an executive of the company. When asked why she was demonstrating, she said, "Blood is no longer thicker than water around here."

TERRY: I never eat any food with additives. I don't eat anything with preservatives or anything that has been sprayed, or anything that has been fed chemical grain.
MARY: And how do you feel?
TERRY: Hungry.

LOUIS: Football players must have a lot of trouble keeping clean.
LESTER: Not so much trouble. Why do you suppose they have a scrub team?

A group of farmers were gathered around the post office window to get their mail when one of them asked the post office clerk, "Any mail for Mike Howe?"
The post office clerk glared over his spectacles and yelled back, "No, no mail for your cow or anybody's cow."

HIRAM: Are you a clock-watcher?
SETH: No. Business is so slow that I watch the calendar.

Two men were flying in an airplane.
Unluckily, one man fell out.
Luckily, there was a haystack under him.
Unluckily, there was a pitchfork in the haystack.
Luckily, he missed the pitchfork.
Unluckily, he missed the haystack.

MOTHER: Would you like some more alphabet soup?
DAUGHTER: No thanks, Mother. I couldn't eat another syllable.

TIM: I saw a baby snake.
JIM: How do you know it was a baby?
TIM: It had a rattle.

GRACE: Where are we eating?
MIKE: Let's eat up the street.
GRACE: Let's not. I hate concrete.

MOTHER: Jimmy, how did you get so dirty?
JIMMY: I'm closer to the ground than you are.

RALPH: Mother, my head is beginning to hurt.
MOTHER: Go take a tonic for it.
RALPH: I have already taken a tonic.
MOTHER: What kind of tonic?
RALPH: Some hair tonic.

"DEAR SANTA CLAUS: I would like a pair of shoes with suction cups so I can stay on the ball."

ALASKAN: Our state is larger than yours.
TEXAN: It won't be when it melts.

KARL: Do you know what a scientist's favorite game is?
STAN: No. What is it?
KARL: Follow the liter.

HE: What did the earth say to the moon?
SHE: "How are your craters?"
HE: What did the moon say to the earth?
SHE: "Oh, they're depressed."

HE: What did the high tide say to the low tide?
SHE: "Lo, tide."
HE: What did the low tide say to the high tide?
SHE: "Hi, tide."
HE: Then what did they say?
SHE: They didn't say anything. They just waved.

SATURN: I bet I get married before you do.
VENUS: Why?
SATURN: I already have a ring.

TERRY: Want to hear the joke about manure?
LARRY: Yes.
TERRY: OK, but don't spread it around.

MOTHER: Why is your baby brother crying?
LESLIE: He dug a hole and wants to bring it into the house.

MYRA: Wow, are you handsome.
MYRON: I wish I could say something nice about you.
MYRA: You could if you lied as well as I do.

Then there was the farmer whose tractor got stuck in reverse and he unplowed fourteen acres.

ISAAC: There is a person in here who thinks he is an owl.
JOEL: Who?

HORRENDOUS: I've invented a computer that's almost human.
GRAVES: You mean it can think?
HORRENDOUS: No. But when it makes a mistake it can put the blame on some other computer.

A man was walking down the street with a grandfather's clock on his back to get it repaired. He wasn't watching where he was going and hit an old lady. She exclaimed, "Sonny, why don't you carry a watch like other people do?"

TOURIST: Has this town got any outstanding sights?
CITIZEN: Oh, yes. We have the biggest helium plant in the world.
TOURIST: Is it in bloom yet?

JANICE: How do you like your new Easter tie?

MIKE: What makes you think it's an Easter tie?
JANICE: It has egg on it.

TOURIST: What a beat-up old shack. What's holding it up?
HERMIT: The termites are holding hands.

HORACE: I hope the rain holds up.
JUDY: Why?
HORACE: Because then it won't come down.

HARRIET: Susan, did you find my sweater?
SUSAN: Was it the red, white, and blue one with the flag on the back and *Bicentennial Year* printed on the front?
HARRIET: Yes. That was it.
SUSAN: No. I didn't find it.

JAN: Eric, is it hard for you to make decisions?
ERIC: Yes . . . and . . . no.

JERRY: What do you have written on your shoe?
MARY: TGIF.
JERRY: What does it stand for?
MARY: Toes go in first.

JARVIS: So you really liked my new dog. I'm glad, because it's a rare breed. It's part boxer and part bull. It cost me two hundred dollars.
CATHY: You must be kidding. Which part is the bull?
JARVIS: The part about the two hundred dollars.

CIRCUS MANAGER (to the human cannonball): You can't quit! Where will I find another man of your caliber?

MAN (standing in the middle of a busy street): Officer, can you tell me how to get to the hospital?
OFFICER: Sure. Just keep standing where you are now.

Why is it that whenever you go fishing, people always ask, "Did you catch those fish?" Well, what do they think—that the fish jumped into the boat and surrendered?

TOM: Why aren't you feeding the birds this year?
CYNTHIA: Last year I spent twenty dollars on birdseed and they still called me "Cheep, cheep."

HARRY: Why did Tom flood the gym?
SANDY: I don't know, why?

HARRY: The coach told him to come in as a sub.

SALLY: What kind of new car did you get?
BUTCH: I can't remember the name of it, but it starts with *T*.
SALLY: Amazing. Most cars I know about start with gasoline.

SON: Dad, give me a dime, please.
FATHER: Son, don't you think you're getting too big to be forever begging for dimes?
SON: I guess you're right, Dad. Please give me a dollar.

CLERK: What's the matter, little boy?
LITTLE BOY (crying): Please, sir, have you seen a lady without a little boy that looks like me?

HUNTER: Look. There's a tiger over there. Is he safe?
GUIDE: He's a lot safer than you are.

DEBBIE: Pretend you have three glasses. Two are filled with water. Does that remind you of a king?
OSCAR: Sure. Phil-Up the Third.

A man was walking on a city sidewalk carrying a typewriter. A lady in a hurry rounded a corner and bumped into him, causing him to drop the typewriter, which was badly damaged.

"Look what you did to my typewriter," said the man.

"Why don't you carry a ballpoint pen like everybody else?" replied the lady.

Jim dropped over to Sam's house for a neighborly chat. Sam, wanting to be a hospitable neighbor, started to pour soda pop into a glass for Jim.

"Say when," instructed Sam.

Sam kept pouring, but Jim showed no sign of saying, "When."

"Did you hear that MacDougal died?" Sam said suddenly.

"When!" yelled Jim.

The human brain is wonderful. It starts working the moment you get up in the morning and doesn't stop until you're called on in class.

STU: There was a robbery in my back yard.
LAURIE: What happened?
STU: Two clothespins held up a pair of pants.

Have you heard about the crossword puzzle addict who died and was buried six feet down and three across?

HOTEL GUEST: How do you expect a fellow to sleep in this awful hotel? Why, I didn't close my eyes all night.
HOTEL DESK CLERK: No wonder you didn't get any rest. Everybody knows you have to close your eyes to go to sleep.

YOUNG MAN: Hey, mister. How did you lose all your hair?
OLD MAN: By worrying.
YOUNG MAN: About what?
OLD MAN: About losing my hair.

TV PRODUCER: I have good news and bad news for you.
TV WRITER: What's the good news?
PRODUCER: ABC and NBC both loved your script, they just ate it up.
WRITER: So what's the bad news?
PRODUCER: ABC and NBC are my dogs' names.

WIFE: You just don't know what I went through to get your birthday present.
HUSBAND: Oh yes, I do—my pockets.

DROWNING MAN: Quick! Throw me a lifesaver!
BOY (on shore): Sure, what flavor? Cherry or peppermint?

Then there was the fellow who tried to blow up the bus, but he burned his lips on the tail pipe.

FATHER: Remember, a job well done never needs to be done again.
SON: What about cutting the grass?

ARNO: Have you ever seen a catfish?
GREG: Sure I have.
ARNO: Oh yeah? Then how do they hold the pole?

MOTHER: Why are your clothes all wet?
LESTER: The label said Wash and Wear.

CATHY: I've seen your face somewhere else.
CARLOS: No, you haven't. It's always been in the same place.

GINNY: I left my watch upstairs.
LENNY: Call it, maybe it will run down.
GINNY: Can't, we have a winding staircase.

SON: Have you ever been to Egypt?
FATHER: No.
SON: Then where did you find my mummy?

LITTLE BROTHER (to gentleman caller): Hi, I knew you were coming to see my sister.
GENTLEMAN CALLER: How did you know that?
LITTLE BOY: I saw my sister hiding the other fellow's picture.

DEBBY: Mom, may I have an apple?
MOTHER: But you just had one.
DEBBY: I know, but an apple a day keeps the doctor away and I just broke his window.

CITY PERSON VISITING A FARM: Hey, these flies are thick around here. Don't you ever shoo them?
FARMER: No, that would be too costly. We let them go barefoot.

Then there were the two guys who went ice fishing. They caught three hundred pounds of ice, cooked it, and drowned.

TEEN-AGER: Hey, Dad, let's buy a new car.
FATHER: Can't you wait until I've had a chance to drive the old one at least once?

BRYAN: I'm glad I wasn't born in France.
CHERYL: Why?
BRYAN: I don't speak French.

HUGH: Did you hear the joke about the roof?
DRAKE: No.
HUGH: Never mind. It's over your head.

DIDI: Did you hear about the fight at the laundry?
GERT: No.
DIDI: The washing machine beat the dirt out of the pants.

TOM: Where did you get that big bump on your head?
MARY: Diving.
TOM: Where did you dive?
MARY: Into the bathtub.

FRED: Are you good at remembering faces, Dad?
DAD: Pretty good, I guess. Why do you ask?
FRED: I just broke your shaving mirror.

MOTHER: Did you thank Mrs. Gordon for the lovely party?
DEENA: No.
MOTHER: Why not?

DEENA: Well, when everybody else thanked her, Mrs. Gordon kept saying, "Don't mention it." So I didn't.

ROCK: I had the radio on last night.
HUDSON: Yeah? Was it a good fit?

LARRY: Did you know that George Washington had wooden false teeth?
HARRY: Yes. And when he took part in a toothpaste test he had fifteen per cent fewer knotholes.

LIBRARIAN: Young man, please be quiet, the people next to you can't read.
BOY: That's too bad. I've been reading since I was six.

KARL: Did you hear about the man who drank furniture polish?
SARAH: Yes. He had a terrible end, but a beautiful finish.

WIFE: I don't want you to buy me something expensive for my birthday. I'd rather have something you made yourself.
HUSBAND: Such as what?
WIFE: Money.

SAUL: Is it OK to go swimming here? I heard there were crocodiles around.
WILL: No, that's a lot of nonsense. The sharks scare them away.

DOCTOR'S SON: My dad's a doctor, so I can get treated for nothing.
AMUSEMENT PARK OWNER'S SON: I can go on the rides for nothing.
MINISTER'S SON: I can be good for nothing.

MAINE FARMER: Our winters are so cold we have to put heaters under the cows to milk them.
GEORGIA FARMER: That's nothing. Our summers are so hot, we have to feed ice to the chickens so they won't lay hard-boiled eggs.

Then there was the forgetful cow who gave milk of amnesia.

WALTER: My sister fell down a flight of stairs.
HIRAM: Cellar?
WALTER: No. I think she can be repaired.

When this fellow's boss went on vacation, he told the boss that he had dreamed that the plane he planned to take had crashed and all on board were killed. The frightened boss took a train, and sure enough the plane did crash and all on board were killed. Several weeks later, the boss had made plans to go on a business trip by car. The employee told the boss that he had dreamed that the bridge on the route the boss planned to take fell into the river. And that is exactly what happened. The boss was safe, because he took a different route, and when he came back he fired the worker for sleeping on the job.

LESTER: Did you catch all those fish by yourself?
NESTOR: No, the worm helped me.

WILL: Did anyone laugh when we fell on the ice?
JILL: No, but the ice made a lot of awful cracks.

COWHAND: You put your saddle on backwards.
DUDE: A lot you know. How do you know which direction I want to go?

JAN: You've got some snew on your face.
MARK: What's snew?
JAN: I don't know, what's new with you?

ARNIE: A nickel, a dime, and a quarter stood on a bridge. The nickel and the dime jumped, but the quarter didn't. Why?
ARABELLA: I don't know. Why?
ARNIE: The quarter had more cents.

A leopard went to the eye doctor for an eye test.
"Whenever I look at my wife, I see spots in front of my eyes," complained the leopard.
"What do you expect," answered the doctor, "you're a leopard."
"Sure," answered the leopard, "but my wife is a zebra."

PETE: I et six eggs for breakfast today.
NELL: You meant *ate*.
PETE: Well, maybe it was eight I et.

JEANETTE: I wouldn't eat those peanuts, they're fattening.
STELLA: How do you know?
JEANETTE: Have you ever seen a skinny elephant?

"Your methods of fruit culture are hopelessly outdated," the young agriculture college graduate said to the old farmer. "I'll be surprised if you get more than two or three bushels of apples from that tree."

"So would I," replied the old farmer. "That's a pear tree."

JACK: That's a peculiar pair of socks you have there—one red and the other yellow.
GENE: I know, and I have another pair at home just like it.

ED: How did you get so tall?
KENNY: I rubbed grease on my head.
ED: I did too, but I didn't get any taller.
KENNY: What did you use?
ED: Crisco.
KENNY: No wonder. That's shortening.

CASPER: My girl wants me to get a job.
RANDALL: What are you looking for?
CASPER: A new girl.

CARLA: Can you tell me the name of an animal that travels great distances but doesn't get very far?
DOLORES: Yes. A goldfish. It swims around the globe.

MORRIS MOUSE: I hope I get to go up in one of those satellites with the monkeys.

MELVILLE MOUSE: Isn't that dangerous?
MORRIS MOUSE: I would prefer it to going back into cancer research.

HORACE: If you're going to do any fishing you have to put the line in the water.
CARL: I can't, the worm can't swim.

Just as the amateur astronomer swung his telescope around, a shooting star fell. A little boy who was watching said, "Say, you're some shot."

BOXER: Do you think I hurt him in that last round?
MANAGER: No, but keep swinging. The breeze might give him pneumonia.

SUSIE: How does a girl keep her youth from slipping away?
TRUDY: Hide his car keys.

MRS. QUINCE: I hear your son writes. Does he write for money?
MRS. FINCH: He certainly does, in every letter he sends to me.

HUSBAND: This coffee tastes like mud.
WIFE: Well, it was just ground this morning.

PILOT: Want a fly?
BOY: Sure I do.
PILOT: I'll catch one for you.

Two men were riding on a train. Each had brought a banana to eat on the trip. Just as they had peeled their bananas, the train went into a tunnel.

"Have you eaten your banana yet?" asked the first man.

"No," said the other. "Why do you ask?"

"Well, I took one bite of mine and I went blind."

YOLANDE: Did you eat cake today?
BRUCE: Why do you ask?
YOLANDE: Your face is crumby.

HARRISON: I understand you solved your son's school lateness problem.
PAXTON: Yes, I bought him a car.
HARRISON: How did that help?
PAXTON: He has to get there early to find a parking space.

TEXAS CITIZEN: We grow cabbages down in Texas three times as big as yours.
IOWA CITIZEN: We make pots three times as big as you make them in Texas.
TEXAS CITIZEN: Why?

IOWA CITIZEN: To cook those big cabbages you grow in Texas.

LEANDER: Why are you so sad?
LUIS: Mom got a new cookie jar.
LEANDER: Why does that make you sad?
LUIS: It plays music when you take the lid off.

MRS. NOSEY: How was the wedding you went to?
LITTLE LIL: The bride changed her mind.
MRS. NOSEY: What do you mean?
LITTLE LIL: She went down the aisle with one man and came back up the aisle with another.

HAROLD: Where's a good place to hunt?
JAMES: Right down the road should be good. I saw a sign that said: "Fine for Hunting."

HUNTER: I spotted a leopard.
COMPANION: Don't be silly. They're born that way.

DEENA: The family next door must be very poor.
DANNY: Why do you say that?
DEENA: You should have heard the fuss they made when the baby swallowed a dime last night.

WIFE: Did you ask your boss for a raise?
HUSBAND: Yes, I did, and he was like a lamb.
WIFE: What did he say?
HUSBAND: Baa.

LYNNE: My grandmother gave me this beautiful wool sweater for my birthday.
GLENN: But the label says cotton.
LYNNE: That's just to fool the moths.

MOTHER: Did you turn off your bedroom light?
SON: I don't know. It's too dark in here for me to see if the switch says on or off.

CATHY: What happened to that stupid brunette your boyfriend used to date?
DEBBIE: I bleached my hair.

JASON: When the company comes, will I have to eat my cake with a fork?
MOTHER: Yes, you will.
JASON: Could I have some to practice on now?

WIFE: Fred! Fred! Wake up. I think I heard a mouse squeak!
SLEEPY HUSBAND: What do you want me to do, get up and oil it?

LARRY (at disco): That blonde dancing over there isn't very smart.
BOB: I know, she hasn't looked at me all night either.

GIRL (at candy counter): Do you take care of the nuts?
CLERK: I wait on anybody.

HOST: If you sleep here tonight, you'll have to make your own bed.
GUEST: That's fine with me.
HOST: Here's a hammer, saw, some glue and nails. You'll find the wood upstairs. Good night.

JOHN: England's national sport is cricket; Spain's national sport is bullfighting.
TIM: I'd rather play in England than in Spain.
JOHN: Why?
TIM: I'd much rather fight a cricket than a bull.

Two little boys were watching the escalator at a department store. One little boy said, "I wonder what happens when the basement gets all full of stairs."

A city girl was on her first visit to the country. She quietly looked at the pigs, cows, chickens, sheep, and horses. But she squealed in delight when she saw the family's pet peacock. "Look," she said, "a rooster in full bloom."

COLLEGE STUDENT: I just got a pet skunk.
ROOMMATE: Where do you think you're going to keep him?
STUDENT: Right here in the dormitory under my bed.
ROOMMATE: What about the smell?
STUDENT: He'll have to get used to it like we did.

BOSS: Why are you carrying only one bag of flour? The other workers are carrying two.
WORKER: Well, I guess they're just too lazy to make two trips the way I do.

HARRY: I hear your daughter's learning to play the harp. How's she doing?
SAM: Well, I don't know, but if that's what the angels play I'm not so sure I want to get to heaven.

VALERIE: So you think you can catch my cold?
VICTOR: I don't know. How fast does it run?

HUSBAND: When I see you in that funny-looking coat I have to laugh.

WIFE: Good. I'll put it on when you get the bill.

MIKE: I saw something last night I'll never get over.
PATTY: What was that?
MIKE: The moon.

A man lost in the African jungle found himself face to face with a lion. He fainted from fright. When he woke up he found the lion was kneeling at his side.
"Thank you for praying for me," said the man, very much relieved that the lion was apparently not going to eat him.
"Sh," said the lion. "I'm saying grace."

Then there was the man who put a "For Sail" sign on his house as it floated down the river during a flood.

MICK: Did you know there's a star called the Dog Star?
STAN: You can't be Sirius.

FATHER: Who gave you that black eye?
SON: No one gave it to me. I had to fight for it.

QUESTION: You are a bus driver. Four people are picked up at one stop. At the next stop eleven people get off and nine people get on. At the stop after that, seven people get on and three get off. Who's driving the bus? ANSWER: *You* are driving the bus.

    SERGEANT: So you're the recruit who's complaining about sand in the soup.
    RECRUIT: That's right, sergeant.
    SERGEANT: Well, when you joined the Army you knew you wouldn't have it as easy as civilian life.
    RECRUIT: That's right, but I joined the Army to serve my country—not eat it.

    TIRED WORKER: This job is getting to me. Every night when I try to get to sleep all I see are snakes and cucumbers.
    FRIEND: Have you seen a doctor?
    WORKER: No, only snakes and cucumbers.

    ANGRY NEIGHBOR: Didn't you hear me pounding on the floor while your party was going on?
    PARTY THROWER: Yes, I did. But that's OK. We were making quite a bit of noise ourselves.

    Two boys had mowed lawns all day, and for their labors they had collected a ten-dollar bill and a five-dollar bill. Joe kept the ten and gave Moe the five.

MOE: You know, if I had done the dividing of the money I would have given you the ten and kept the five. That's the nice thing to do.
JOE: So what are you complaining about?

TED: How would you like to make a hundred dollars?
FRED: Sure. What do I have to do?
TED: Just do a little worrying for us.
FRED: When do I get the hundred dollars?
TED: That's your first worry.

On his way home from work a man saw a twenty-dollar bill on the sidewalk. He stooped to pick it up and a voice out of nowhere boomed, "This is the voice of Daniel Boone. Taking that money will spell your doom."

So the man left the money. Four more people who saw the money received the same message and left the money there. A fifth person, however, said upon hearing the message, "Oh yeah. This is the voice of Davy Crockett and that twenty goes in my pocket."

MAN: Does your dog bite?
BOY: No, sir.
MAN (after petting the dog and being bitten): I thought you said your dog didn't bite.
BOY: That's not my dog.

RITA: Our dog's coat is so thick the summer heat bothers him.
ZITA: Why don't you take it off for the summer?
RITA: I would but I can't find the zipper.

A little boy was watching his first ballet. He watched with great interest as the dancers danced on their toes. "Why don't they just get taller dancers, Mommy?" he asked.

GRANDSON: Is TV really an improvement over radio, Granddad?
GRANDDAD: Certainly is; not only can you hear the static, you can see it.

EMPLOYEE: Could I have tomorrow off, so I can help with the spring cleaning at home?
BOSS: Not tomorrow, I'm afraid. There are too many important things to do.
EMPLOYEE: Oh, thank you. I knew I could count on you.

"Will you pass the nuts, please?" said the dinner guest to the absentminded professor.
"Oh, I suppose so," said the professor. "But I really should fail the lot of them."

A man was reading a book in the park. Every minute or so he would tear out a page, fold it neatly, and put it under the park bench.

"Why are you doing that?" asked a passerby.

"To keep the aardvarks away," said the reader.

"I don't see any aardvarks," said the passerby.

"Effective, isn't it?" replied the reader.

VIRGIL: What would you do if you were in my shoes?

VERA: Polish them.

BEGGAR: Could you spare five dollars for a cup of coffee?

PASSERBY: Coffee doesn't cost that much.

BEGGAR: I'm a big tipper.

The detective was investigating the jewelry robbery.

DETECTIVE: Can you tell me what happened?

CLERK: A motorcycle pulled up. An elephant jumped off, came in and pointed a machine gun at us, and demanded the jewels.

DETECTIVE: Can you describe the suspect?

CLERK: You know what an elephant looks like.

DETECTIVE: There are two kinds of elephants, African, with big ears, and Indian, with small ears. What kind was this elephant?

CLERK: How should I know? He had pulled a stocking cap over his head!

Then there was the fellow who wouldn't go out with his wife because he was already married.

There were three shipwrecked men in a lifeboat in the middle of the ocean. All they had left to eat between them was one slice of salami. They agreed that whoever had the best dream would get the salami. The next morning the first man said, "I dreamed I was a big shipping executive, owning thousands of ships, and that we were rescued by one of my ships."
The second man said, "I dreamed that I thought of a way to teleportate people to distant planets."
The third man said, "I dreamed that both of you fell overboard so I got up and ate the salami."

LOUISE: I spend hours in front of the mirror admiring my beauty. Is that vanity?
IRENE: No, it's your imagination.

JOE: Did you hear the joke about the jump rope?
MOE: No.
JOE: Skip it.

CITY BOY: Look at that bunch of cows!
FARM BOY: No. Herd.
CITY BOY: Heard of what?
FARM BOY: Herd of cows.
CITY BOY: Of course I've heard of cows.
FARM BOY: No, a cow herd.
CITY BOY: What did the cow hear?

The saloon door flew open and the cowboy came flying out and hit the dusty street.
"Did they throw you out?" asked a passerby.
"No," said the cowboy, "but I sure would like to find the polecat who moved my horse."

HORACE: What do you think of our little town?
MORRIS: It's very nicely laid out. How long has it been dead?

SON: Dad, I'd like to study the stars when I grow up.
RICH FATHER: Certainly, son, and I'll buy Hollywood and Beverly Hills for you, too.

MRS. GRIMES (to garbageman): Am I too late for the garbage?
GARBAGEMAN: No m'am, jump right in.

HARRY: I have an uncle in Alaska.
BARRY: Nome?

HARRY: Of course I know him.
BARRY: No, I mean Nome in Alaska.
HARRY: He's in the family. I'd know him anywhere.

VALERIE: My new boyfriend is so romantic; he's always saying "fair lady" to me.
GLORIA: Romantic, my eye. He's training to be a bus driver.

BOY ESKIMO: What would you say if I braved a fierce storm, and went through hundreds of miles of ice and snow, and fought off polar bears, and nearly drowned on the ice floes, as I pushed my dog team onward and onward to bring the new medicine to save the dying child?
GIRL ESKIMO: I'd say that was a lot of mush.

NEIGHBOR: Were you playing the saxophone last night?
BUDDING MUSICIAN: Yes, I was.
NEIGHBOR: Would you play a solo tonight?
MUSICIAN: Solo?
NEIGHBOR: Yes. Play so low I can't hear it.

MACK: Windy today, isn't it?
ZACK: No, it's Thursday, I think.
MACK: So am I. Let's go get a drink.

LARRY: I started out in life without a nickel in my pocket.
JERRY: I started out in life without a pocket.

JACK: I hear your brother got his driver's license. Does he know much about cars?
MACK: No, he thinks you cool the engine by stripping the gears.

DICK: Did you know that a grasshopper can jump four times its length?
MARY: No, but I once saw a little bee lift a two-hundred-pound man four feet off the ground.

PHONE CALLER: Hello, is this 846-3731?
ANSWERER: No, this is 946-3731.
CALLER: Sorry to have bothered you.
ANSWERER: That's OK. I had to get up to answer the phone anyway.

DEBBIE: Why can't you thread the needle?
LUCY: Every time I get the thread close to the needle the eye blinks.

MOTHER: Be sure to wash your arms before you put on a clean shirt.
SON: Long or short sleeves?

The proud sixteen-year-old had passed his driving test. He then told his three younger brothers and sisters, "You can all move up one bike now."

MOTHER (hearing crash in kitchen): More dishes, dear?
HUSBAND: No, dear. Less dishes.

ED: What are you doing?
EDNA: Writing a letter to Cousin John.
ED: Why are you writing so slowly?
EDNA: He can't read very fast.

LUMBERJACK ZEKE: It was so cold where I was cutting timber that the candle froze and we couldn't blow it out.
LUMBERJACK MACK: That's nothing. Where I was hauling timber it was so cold that when we talked our words froze in midair, and we had to take them in the cabin and fry them so we'd know what we said.

WIFE: When are you going to fix the fence?
HUSBAND: When Junior comes home from college for the holidays.
WIFE: Why are you waiting until then?
HUSBAND: Junior can be a big help. Don't you know he's on the fencing team?

AUNTIE EMILY: Were you a good little girl in church today?
LITTLE GIRL: Yes, I was. A man was passing around a tray of money and I didn't take any.

DRIVING TEACHER: If there is any kind of emergency, put on the emergency brake.
STUDENT: Doesn't that come already installed?

UNION LEADER: We're going to strike.
WORKER: What for?
UNION LEADER: Shorter hours.
WORKER: That's good. I always did think sixty minutes was too long for an hour.

MOTHER: Have you filled the saltshaker yet?
DAUGHTER: No, Mother, it's hard to get the salt in through those little holes.

WIFE: Have you seen the new sieve?
HUSBAND: I took it back to the store.
WIFE: Why?
HUSBAND: It was no good. It was full of holes.

Two carpenters were working on a building. One kept examining nails and throwing most of them away.
"Why are you throwing so many nails away?" asked his co-worker.

"They're pointed the wrong way. The head's on the wrong side of the nail," answered the carpenter.

"Don't throw those away," countered the other carpenter. "Those are for the other side of the building."

TEEN-AGER: Could I have the car tonight, Dad?

FATHER: What do you have two legs for?

TEEN-AGER: One is for the gas pedal, the other is for the brake pedal.

BROTHER: I thought I asked you not to tell Mother how late I came in!

SISTER: I didn't. I said I was too busy making breakfast when you came in to notice you.

The parents, who had not been fortunate enough to get an education themselves, sent their son to a very exclusive and expensive school. When the boy returned, the parents sometimes had trouble understanding the big words their son used, but they were eager to learn. One evening as the son was reading a book, the mother asked, "What are you reading, son?"

"A narrative," replied the son.

"What's a narrative?" the mother asked.

"A narrative is a tale," said the son.

A little later the son said, "Mother, would you please extinguish the light. I forgot."
"What does that mean?" asked the mother.
"Extinguish means to put out."
A few days later, the parents held a dinner party in honor of their son. The family dog came into the dining room and started to bark and annoy the guests, whereupon the mother said, "Son, will you please take the dog by his narrative and extinguish him."

FATHER (to son while on a car trip): Look, there's a Jersey cow.
SON: How did you know, Dad? I didn't see the license plate.

BOASTING BOY: My father has George Washington's watch.
BOASTING GIRL: That's nothing. My father has Adam's apple.

JULIETTE: I went riding this morning.
HARRIET: Horseback?
JULIETTE: Oh sure, he got back more than two hours ago.

DIRECTOR: Do you have any acting experience?
BUDDING ACTOR: My leg was in a cast once.

NEIGHBOR: Do you have to make so much noise?
NEIGHBORHOOD KID: I can't play tennis without a racket.

Two kids were talking about parents.
"My parents do things backwards," said one.
"How's that?" said the other.
"When I'm wide awake and not tired they send me to bed. When I'm sleepy in the morning they wake me up."

BOSS: I need a responsible person for this job.
JOB APPLICANT: Then I'm the right person for you. Every place I worked, whenever anything went wrong, they said I was responsible.

CARPENTER: You hammer like lightning.
CARPENTER'S HELPER: You mean I'm fast?
CARPENTER: No. I mean you never hit the same place twice.

HIKER: If I cut through your field, will I get to the bus depot in time to catch the four o'clock bus?
FARMER: If my bull sees you, you'll catch the three o'clock bus.

Then there were the two mosquitoes having a chat on Robinson Crusoe's back. One said to the other, "I have to go now, but let's meet again on Friday."

STEVE: Did you hear about the fight in the candy store?
CLEVE: No. What happened?
STEVE: The lollipop got licked.

The young man at the singles dance said to the girl, "Are you unattached?"
"No," answered the girl. "I'm just put together carelessly."

BOSS: Did the foreman tell you what to do?
NEW WORKER: Yes, sir. He said to wake him up when I saw you coming.

LINDA: Whenever I'm down in the dumps, I get a new dress.
SHIRLEY: From the looks of the one you're wearing, that must be where you got it.

The two riders on the bicycle built for two had a hard time getting to the top of the hill. When they finally made it, one said to the other, "Whew, that was tough. I didn't think we were going to make it."
"It was hard alright," said the other. "It's a good thing I kept the brakes on or we would have rolled back down the hill."

FATHER: Why are you crying, son?
SON: I cleaned the bird cage and the canary disappeared.
FATHER: How did you clean it?
SON: With the vacuum cleaner.

PASSENGER: Please slow down. I get nervous when you turn corners so fast.
TAXI DRIVER: Do what I do, lady. Close your eyes.

ANN: My dog is a baseball dog.
STAN: What makes him a baseball dog?
ANN: He catches flies, chases fowls, and beats it for for home when he sees the catcher coming.

The cabbage, the tomato, and the faucet were entered in the big race. The race started and the TV announcer called the race: "Cabbage is ahead, tomato is trying to catch up, and the game little faucet is still running."

Two visitors to a museum were looking at an Egyptian mummy labeled, "3500 B.C."
"What does the sign mean?" asked one visitor.
"That's probably the license plate number of the car that hit him," answered the other.

MARK: What do you think of the new telephone book?
WENDY: Well, it doesn't have much plot, but it certainly has a lot of characters.

Two ants were running across the top of a cereal box. One stopped and said to the other, "Hey, why are we running so fast?"
"Didn't you read what it says here?" answered the other ant. "Tear across dotted line."

Then there was the man who bought a new mousetrap but forgot to buy cheese for bait. He put a picture of a piece of cheese on the trap. When he checked the trap the next morning, he found that he had caught a picture of a mouse.

GUARD: Halt! You can't go in there.
PRIVATE: Why not?
GUARD: That's the general's tent.
PRIVATE: Then why does that sign on the door say, "Private"?

VICKY: Did you know it takes five sheep to make one sweater?
RICKY: That's interesting. I didn't know they could knit.

SINGER: Did you notice how my voice filled the theater tonight?
FRIEND: Yes. I even noticed people leaving to make room for it.

JIM: Did you hear about the accident at the army base?
HAL: Yeah. A jeep ran over a box of popcorn and killed two kernels.

SAM: Why are you standing in front of the mirror with your eyes closed?
SAL: I want to see what I look like when I'm asleep.

JERRY: Why couldn't Robin play in the baseball game?
SARAH: He didn't have a bat, man.

GRANDFATHER: What are you going to be when you finish school?
GRANDSON: Older than you.

A hen and a pig were walking down the road. They saw a sign in front of a restaurant: "Special today—Ham and Eggs."

The hen said, "I'm proud to see that sign."

"Easy for you to talk," said the pig. "All you have to do is make a donation. I have to make the supreme sacrifice."

JOHN: Why does it take a baseball player longer to run from second to third base than it does to run between other bases?
LON: I don't know, why?
JOHN: There's a short stop between.

GERT: Let's buy a hot dog.
MYRT: I better not. Mother and I are on a diet.
GERT: Who's lost the most weight?
MYRT: Father.

Joey came home from school with a bloody nose and a black eye.
"You've been fighting again," said his mother. "Didn't I tell you to count to fifty before you started to fight?"
"You sure did," answered Joey, "but Tommy's mother told him to count to twenty-five."

The little girl's sniffling annoyed the lady who was sitting next to her in a movie theater.
"Don't you have a handkerchief, young lady?" the lady asked.
"Yes, but my mother won't let me lend it to anybody," replied the girl.

JOHN: Do you think anybody can predict the future with cards?
JOAN: My mother can. She takes one look at

my report card and tells me what my father will do when he sees it.

    COACH: OK, Chuck. Get in there and get ferocious.
    PLAYER: Sure, coach. What's his number?

    MUCK: How did you get that red spot on your nose?
    MIRE: From smelling a brose.
    MUCK: There's no *b* in rose.
    MIRE: There was in this one.

    MRS. A: Why are you knitting three socks?
    MRS. B: My son wrote me that he grew another foot since he went to camp.

    JOHN: My mother treats me like a god.
    JOAN: How does she do that?
    JOHN: She gives me burnt offerings at every meal.

    HARRY: Did you get an invitation to Beth's party?
    LARRY: Yes, but I can't go. The invitation says from two to five, and I'm past seven.

    SARAH: I tried to call the zoo and can't.
    BELLE: Why?
    SARAH: The lion's busy.

HAL: How do you catch a squirrel?
MAL: How?
HAL: Climb a tree and act like a nut.

MOTHER: Ned, I told you to share the sled with your little brother.
NED: I am, Mom. I have it downhill and he has it uphill.

A little boy was closely watching a moving escalator. A clerk asked, "Anything wrong, son?"

"No," he answered. "I'm only waiting for my bubble gum to come back."

WIFE: How are we going to observe our anniversary?
HUSBAND: How about a moment of silence?

BOSS: Didn't you receive my letter saying you were fired?
WORKER: Yes, I did, but "return in five days" was written on the envelope.

TINA (to friend on a scale): Are you gaining weight?
LISA: No. According to the chart I should be three inches taller.

An army sergeant was training a new bunch of recruits. "When I give the order," he said, "fire at will."

Suddenly one of the recruits ran away.

"What's the matter with him?" demanded the sergeant.

"That was Will," answered one of the recruits.

The lady opened her refrigerator and found a rabbit in there. "What are you doing there?" she asked.

"Westing," answered the rabbit.

"Why in the refrigerator?" she demanded.

"This is a Westinghouse, isn't it?" answered the rabbit.

JAKE: My great-grandfather was in the Civil War.

RAY: He couldn't have been. He was only a baby then.

JAKE: He was in the infantry.

JAN: The last time I went horseback riding the horse wanted to go one way and I wanted to go another way.

BILL: So what happened?

JAN: The horse tossed me for it.

EAGER FOOTBALL PLAYER: Are you going to let me play in the big game, coach?

COACH: Yes, you're going to be left end.

PLAYER: Left end?

COACH: Right. Sit on the left end of the bench to keep it tilting up when players leave it.

MR. GRIMES: I hear your daughter is getting married. Is she prepared for the battle of life?
MRS. HINES: I think so, she's already been in three engagements.

MARLENE: The moon is going broke.
JEFF: Why do you say that?
MARLENE: The TV weather person says the moon is down to its last quarter.

LARRY: I found fifty cents on the sidewalk.
TERRY: It must be mine, I lost a half-dollar yesterday.
LARRY: But I found two quarters.
TERRY: It must have broke when it hit the sidewalk.

JUDY: You say your brother was kicked out of the Navy just because he likes to sleep with the windows open?
JERRY: He was in the submarine service.

PAPA KANGAROO: Where's Junior?
MOTHER KANGAROO: He's gone. Someone must have picked my pocket.

FATHER: When I was your age I thought nothing of walking fifteen miles to school.
SON: I wouldn't think much of it either.

KEN: Did you hear about the fish I almost caught?
LEN: No, what about it?
KEN: It was almost five feet long, and must have weighed over fifty pounds. I never saw such a fish!
LEN: I believe you.

HAROLD: Do you find writing to be a thankless job?
SUSAN: Not at all. Everything I write is returned to me with thanks.

A man fell out of a second-story window. A crowd gathered soon after he hit the sidewalk. A person bent down and asked, "What happened?"
"I don't know," answered the fall victim, "I just got here."

REPORTER: How did you win the Medal of Honor?
COMMANDING OFFICER: I saved the lives of everyone in my regiment.
REPORTER: How did you do that?
COMMANDING OFFICER: I had the cook transferred.

DRIVER: I'm sorry I ran over your pig. I'll replace it.
FARMER: You can't, you're not fat enough.

MOTHER: Every time you're bad you give me another gray hair.
SON: You must have been a terror, Mom. Look at Grandma!

The cabdriver saw two repairmen climb a pole just as he rounded the bend. "Look at them," he said. "They must think I'm a new driver."

INTERVIEWER: What makes you think you're a good comedian?
FAMOUS COMEDIAN: I threw some of my jokes into the fire and the fire roared.

A driver was following a taillight in a very thick fog, when suddenly the car he was following stopped and he crashed into it.
"Why don't you signal when you stop?" yelled the surprised motorist.
"Why should I?" answered the other driver. "I'm in my own garage."

The nervous passenger asked, "Do ships like this sink very often?"

"Not at all," answered the captain. "They only sink once."

VISITOR: Are your parents in?
BOY: They was in, but they is out now.
VISITOR: Where's your grammar?!
BOY: She's in the kitchen making cookies.

JOHN: I almost drowned when the boat capsized. As I went down for the third time I saw my whole life flash before me.
JIM: Did you see the time I lent you five dollars?

VISITOR: My, my, look at the clock. Is it that late? I had better be going.
LITTLE BOY: You don't have to be in such a hurry. Daddy pushed the clock an hour ahead before you came over.

Little Laurie was left to fix lunch. When her mother returned home with a friend, she noticed that Laurie had already strained the tea.

"Did you find the tea strainer?" she asked Laurie.

"No, Mom, but I used the fly swatter."

Her mother nearly fainted, so Laurie hastily said, "Don't faint, Mom. I used the old one."

A son's letter from summer camp:
Dear Mom and Dad,
I have joined the boxing club. This morning I had my first fight. I don't think I'll need braces for my teeth any more.

HESTER: The minister had the mailbox removed from in front of his church.
LESTER: Why?
HESTER: It had a sign that read, "No Collections on Sunday."

EVE: They say that carrots are good for your eyes. How can you prove it?
ERNEST: Have you ever seen a rabbit wear glasses?

FARMER GRIMES: Quite a storm we had last night.
FARMER SNEED: Yep.
FARMER GRIMES: Damage your barn?
FARMER SNEED: Dunno. Haven't found it yet.

A hobo called at a farm home and asked for food.
"Would you like a chop?" asked the farmer's wife.
"That depends," said the hobo. "Do you mean lamb, pork, or wood?"

A man was sitting at a bar and crying.

"What's the matter?" asked a concerned bystander.

"Rockefeller's dead," blubbered the crying man.

"Was Rockefeller related to you?" asked the bystander.

"No. And that's why I'm crying."

Things That Go Bump in the Night

BUDDY: What has four feet, two heads, four arms, and flies.
MUDDY: Two witches.

How does the zombie play poker?
ANSWER: With a deadpan.

Why didn't the skeleton dance at the senior prom?
ANSWER: He had no body to dance with.

What's the vampire's favorite animal?
ANSWER: A giraffe.

What kind of car does a vampire drive?
ANSWER: A bloodmobile.

Why was the witch first in the class?
ANSWER: She was the best speller.

Why does Dracula help young vampires?
ANSWER: Because he wants to see new blood in the business.

An American newspaper reporter traveling in England dropped into a pub for a bit of refreshment. He walked up to the bar and saw, to his great astonishment, a six-inch-high man standing on the bar drinking beer out of a thimble-sized mug. The man was dressed in the full dress uniform of a major in the British Army right down to a two-inch swagger stick tucked under his arm.

"Why, this is absolutely remarkable," sputtered the reporter. "Have you always been like this?"

"No, and I don't care to talk about it. Thank you," answered the major.

"Oh, but please," pleaded the reporter. "This would make a great story. I'm sure that what you have to say is quite fascinating."

"I don't care to talk about it," the major snapped.

"This would be the greatest story of my career," said the reporter. "I'd share the money with you."

The major just turned his back and drank his beer.

"Oh, come on, major," said the bartender as he dried glasses. "Give the young American feller a break. Tell him how you told off that bloomin' witch doctor."

I was sitting on a tombstone
When a ghost came up and said,
"I'm sorry to disturb you,
But you're sitting on my head."

    HE: What do baby ghosts drink?
    SHE: Evaporated milk.

    MARK: What did one casket say to the other casket?

TOD: I don't know.
MARK: Is that you coffin?

SAM: Sandy, how do ghosts like their eggs?
SANDY: Terrifried.

FIRST GHOST: I feel faint.
SECOND GHOST: I believe it. You are as white as a sheet.

DRACULA: I want to drink your blood.
VICTIM: I gave at the office.

JACK: How does Dracula make a jail?
LEE: With blood cells.

FRANKENSTEIN'S MONSTER: What lovely eyes you have.
MONSTER'S GIRL FRIEND: Thank you. They were a birthday present.

JANET: Which monster likes to race?
JOANNA: Drag-ula.

FIRST MUMMY: You know that big statue of a crouching lion with a human head that stands near the pyramids? Well, its nose is broken off.
SECOND MUMMY: Really? Then how does it smell?
FIRST MUMMY: Smell? It sphinx.

DEBBIE: I think our school is haunted.
GLORIA: What makes you think that?
DEBBIE: I always hear people talking about the school spirit.

What do ghosts eat on a picnic?
ANSWER: BOO-logna.

What happened when the Frankenstein monster asked the girl monster for her hand in marriage?
ANSWER: That's all he got.

What happens if you cross a werewolf with a computer?
ANSWER: Either an electric fur coat or a machine that bites.

What happens when you cross a mummy with a vampire?
ANSWER: Either a flying Band-Aid or a gift-wrapped bat.

There were three witches that all looked alike. A man called one witch and all of them came. What did he say then?
"Which witch are you?"

MARY: What advice does a mother Halloween ghost give her children?
STEPHANIE: Spook when you're spooken to.

CHARLOTTE: What do demons have that nobody else has?
ANN: Baby demons.

STANLEY: What does a ghost on duty say when he hears a noise?
LEILA: Who ghost there?

We understand that Dr. Frankenstein sent his monster's skeleton package from Transylvania by Tarsal Post.

WARREN: What would you do if you saw Frankenstein's monster, the Mummy, and the Wolf Man?
KATIE: Hope it is Halloween.

WALTER: What did the mother ghost say to the baby ghost when they got in the car?
LORRAINE: Fasten your sheet belt.

PETE: What kind of beans do werewolves like?
TOM: What kind?
PETE: Human beans.

HOWARD: What did one mummy say to the other?
HAROLD: I don't know.
HOWARD: I'm all tied up.

BOB: When is a mummy not a mummy?
RENNIE: When it's a daddy.

PHILIP: What did the ghost have for dessert?
RACHEL: Booberry pie.

Why did the vampire break up with his girl friend?
ANSWER: Because she wasn't his type.

Why did the vampire's girl friend break up with the vampire?
ANSWER: Because he was a pain in the neck.

What do ghosts eat at a beach picnic?
ANSWER: Sand-witches.

Where did the ghosts demonstrate about high taxes?
ANSWER: At the BOO-ston Tea Party.

What does Dracula do with Listerscream mouthwash?
ANSWER: He gargoyles with it.

Why didn't Frankenstein's monster win the Mr. America contest?
ANSWER: He had too many imported parts.

The ghost couldn't make the school football team, so what did he do to help the team?
ANSWER: He became a BOOster.

Why did Dracula always fail arithmetic tests when he was in school?
ANSWER: Because he never wrote down the plus signs.

What did the vampire say when he was asked to dinner?
ANSWER: "No fangs, I just ate."

What do ghosts do to amuse themselves?
ANSWER: They tell people stories.

Dr. Frankenstein sent Igor to get two fresh bodies. Igor went to the cemetery and dug up two bodies from a grave marked "John and Grace Hill." While Dr. Frankenstein worked on the bodies he asked Igor to get some music on the radio. As soon as the music started, the two bodies came to life and got up from the table.
Igor said, "The Hills are alive with the sound of music."

What do ghosts have for dinner?
ANSWER: SPOOK-ghetti.

The vampire took an ocean cruise. He went into the dining room and said, "I'm starving."
"Would you like to see a menu?" asked the waiter.
"No, just show me the passenger list," answered the vampire.

Where does a ghost keep his car?
ANSWER: In a mirage.

Why did the vampire walk around in his pajamas?
ANSWER: He didn't have a bat robe.

What was the first thing the vampire asked to see on his visit to New York City?
ANSWER: The Vampire State Building.

What did one ghost say to the other?
ANSWER: Do you believe in people?

Dracula was lying in his coffin sleeping one bright, sunny day. For a prank some boys nailed roller skates to the coffin and sent it rolling down a hill. It narrowly missed people and cars and went crashing through a drugstore window. As the coffin sped through the drugstore the startled pharmacist heard Dracula say, "You got anything to help stop this coffin?"

What do you call a friendly, handsome Wolf Man?
ANSWER: A failure.

Knock Knock Jokes

Knock, knock.
Who's there?
Dwaine.
Dwaine who?
Dwaine the bathtub, I'm dwowning!

Knock, knock.
Who's there?
Little old lady.
Little old lady who?
I didn't know you could yodel!

Knock, knock.
Who's there?
Ron.
Ron who?
Ron faster! There's a bull after us.

Knock, knock.
Who's there?
Dennis.
Dennis who?
Dennis the room where I keep my books.

Knock, knock.
Who's there?
Flo.
Flo who?
Flo ride is good for your teeth.

Knock, knock.
Who's there?
Stephan.
Stephan who?
Stephan my toe and I'll holler.

Knock, knock.
Who's there?
Conrad.
Conrad who?
Conrad the whole book.

Knock, knock.
Who's there?
Yvonne.
Yvonne who?
Yvonne to be alone.

Knock, knock.
Who's there?
Howard.
Howard who?
Howard you today?

Knock, knock.
Who's there?
Arlo.
Arlo who?
Arlo vans better than high vans?

Knock, knock.
Who's there?
Ivan.
Ivan who?
Ivan holds more than a low van.

Knock, knock.
Who's there?
Truman.
Truman who?
Truman is better than a false one.

Knock, knock.
Who's there?
Bruno.
Bruno who?
Bruno witches' brews here.

Knock, knock.
Who's there?
Heinz.
Heinz who?
Heinz sight is better than foresight.

Knock, knock.
Who's there?
Julian.
Julian who?
Julian David are married.

Knock, knock.
Who's there?
Arnon.
Arnon who?
Arnon of you coming to the party?

Knock, knock.
Who's there?
Osten.
Osten who?
Osten questions and you might get one answer.

Knock, knock.
Who's there?
Nicolette.
Nicolette who?
Nicolette me use the car.

Knock, knock.
Who's there?
Dwight.
Dwight who?
Dwight way is better than sevewal wong ways.

Knock, knock.
Who's there?
Theresa.
Theresa who?
Theresa nice to plant but they take a long time to grow.

Knock, knock.
Who's there?
Lyman.

Lyman who?
Lyman, and you will be caught in your lie.

Knock, knock.
Who's there?
Obadiah.
Obadiah who?
Obadiah is where you'll find it.

Knock, knock.
Who's there?
Hans.
Hans who?
Hans off my property.

Knock, knock.
Who's there?
Dexter.
Dexter who?
Dexter what floors are called in the Navy.

Knock, knock.
Who's there?
Wiley.
Wiley who?
Wiley the hours away.

Knock, knock.
Who's there?
Mark.

Mark who?
Mark my word, these knock knock jokes will be outlawed.

Knock, knock.
Who's there?
Barbara.
Barbara who?
Barbara a cup of sugar for me please.

Knock, knock.
Who's there?
Lois.
Lois who?
Lois the dachshund to the ground.

Knock, knock.
Who's there?
Hatch.
Hatch who?
Gesundheit!

Knock, knock.
Who's there?
Dunbar.
Dunbar who?
Dunbar me from entering.

Knock, knock.
Who's there?

Reed.
Reed who?
Reed books instead of watching TV.

Knock, knock.
Who's there?
Ray.
Ray who?
Ray team ray!

Knock, knock.
Who's there?
Popeye.
Popeye who?
Popeye've got to have the car tonight.

Knock, knock.
Who's there?
Lettuce.
Lettuce who?
Lettuce in, we're freezing out here.

Knock, knock.
Who's there?
Orange.
Orange who?
Orange you glad I'm here?

Knock, knock.
Who's there?

Doughnut.
Doughnut who?
Doughnut open until Christmas.

Knock, knock.
Who's there?
Gus.
Gus who?
Gus who's coming for dinner?

Knock, knock.
Who's there?
Manuel.
Manuel who?
Manuel transmission's harder to drive than automatic.

Knock, knock.
Who's there?
Phillip.
Phillip who?
Phillip the tank, please.

Knock, knock.
Who's there?
Esther.
Esther who?
Esther no questions, she'll tell you no lies.

Malcolm.
Malcolm who?
Malcolm over to see me some time.

Knock, knock.
Who's there?
Moshe.
Moshe who?
Moshe on over here and let's palaver.

Knock, knock.
Who's there?
Marcel.
Marcel who?
Marcel me a new car.

Knock, knock.
Who's there?
Lucille.
Lucille who?
Lucille the envelope and mail it.

Knock, knock.
Who's there?
Hoo.
Hoo who?
I never knew you were an owl.

Knock, knock.
Who's there?

Just Diane.
Just Diane who?
Just Diane to see you.

Knock, knock.
Who's there?
Harry.
Harry who?
Harry up, I'm waiting.

Knock, knock.
Who's there?
Cantaloupe.
Cantaloupe who?
Cantaloupe tonight, Dad's got the car.

Knock, knock.
Who's there?
Carlos.
Carlos who?
Carlos? Call the insurance company.

Knock, knock.
Who's there?
Owen.
Owen who?
Owen money—pay up.

Knock, knock.
Who's there?

Hugh.
Hugh who?
Hugh the wood and carry the water.

Knock, knock.
Who's there?
Claude.
Claude who?
Claude my way through a crowd to get here.

Knock, knock.
Who's there?
Byron.
Byron who?
Byron. See you later.

Knock, knock.
Who's there?
Chester.
Chester who?
Chester your back hurt?

Knock, knock.
Who's there?
Luther.
Luther who?
Luther the thkate, the harder it ith to roll.

Knock, knock.
Who's there?

Aristotle.
Aristotle who?
Aristotle over here and get some candy.

Knock, knock.
Who's there?
Colin.
Colin who?
Colin on you to see how you are.

Knock, knock.
Who's there?
Roland.
Roland who?
Roland along my happy way.

Knock, knock.
Who's there?
Lista.
Lista who?
Lista complaints about you here.

Knock, knock.
Who's there?
Benjamin.
Benjamin who?
Benjamin around in my hot rod.

Knock, knock.
Who's there?

Yule.
Yule who?
Yule come on down, you hear?

Knock, knock.
Who's there?
Lyle.
Lyle who?
Lyle away the hours.

Knock, knock.
Who's there?
Vincent.
Vincent who?
Vincent me over here.

Knock, knock.
Who's there?
Rudy.
Rudy who?
Rudy day knock knock jokes got started.

Knock, knock.
Who's there?
Barry.
Barry who?
Barry me not on the lone prairie.

Knock, knock.
Who's there?

Sir.
Sir who?
Sir-prize.

Knock, knock.
Who's there?
Sarah.
Sarah who?
Sarah doctor in the house?

Knock, knock.
Who's there?
Turner.
Turner who?
Turner round and go home.

Knock, knock.
Who's there?
Boo.
Boo who?
You don't have to cry about it.

Knock, knock.
Who's there?
I know.
I know who?
If you know, then why do you ask?

Knock, knock.
Who's there?

Jess.
Jess who?
Jess little old me!

Knock, knock.
Who's there?
Debbie.
Debbie who?
Debbie or not Debbie, that is the question.

Knock, knock.
Who's there?
Salvatore.
Salvatore who?
Salvatore the paper to shreds.

Knock, knock.
Who's there?
Decode.
Decode who?
Decode air outside is freezing my ears.

Knock, knock.
Who's there?
Shelby.
Shelby who?
Shelby coming around the mountain when she comes.

Knock, knock.
Who's there?

Isabel.
Isabel who?
Isabel necessary on a fire truck?

Knock, knock.
Who's there?
Rita.
Rita who?
Rita good book lately?

Knock, knock.
Who's there?
Ibin.
Ibin who?
Ibin waiting here for ages for you to open the door.

Knock, knock.
Who's there?
Harriet.
Harriet who?
Harriet all the food, and there was none left for us.

Knock, knock.
Who's there?
Wendy.
Wendy who?
Wendy today, rainy tomorrow.

Knock, knock.
Who's there?
Anita.
Anita who?
Anita new tire for my bike.

Knock, knock.
Who's there?
Denise.
Denise who?
Denise knows me. The nephew doesn't.

Knock, knock.
Who's there?
Freeze.
Freeze who?
Freeze a jolly good fellow.

Knock, knock.
Who's there?
Sharon.
Sharon who?
Sharon share alike.

Knock, knock.
Who's there?
Les.
Les who?
Les cut out these silly knock knock jokes.

Knock, knock.
Who's there?
Andrew.
Andrew who?
Andrew a picture of a horse.

Knock, knock.
Who's there?
Gail.
Gail who?
Gail winds kicking up.

Knock, knock.
Who's there?
Ida.
Ida who?
Ida clare these knock knock jokes are silly.

Knock, knock.
Who's there?
Lena.
Lena who?
Lena on the bell and it will ring.

Knock, knock.
Who's there?
Hiram.
Hiram who?
Hiram today and fire 'em tomorrow.

Knock, knock.
Who's there?
Frank Lee.
Frank Lee who?
Frank Lee I think we've had enough knock knock jokes.

Knock, knock.
Who's there?
Hyman.
Hyman who?
Hyman, what's new and groovy?

Knock, knock.
Who's there?
Marion.
Marion who?
Marion is what leads to divorcin'.

Knock, knock.
Who's there?
Theodore.
Theodore who?
Theodore is stuck and I can't get in.

Knock, knock.
Who's there?
José.
José who?
José can you see by the dawn's early light?

Knock, knock.
Who's there?
Denial.
Denial who?
Denial is a river in Egypt.

Knock, knock.
Who's there?
Kent.
Kent who?
Kent you tell who it is?

Knock, knock.
Who's there?
Della.
Della who?
Della Katessen.

Knock, knock.
Who's there?
Stan.
Stan who?
Stan up and be counted.

Knock, knock.
Who's there?
Deadeye.
Deadeye who?
Deadeye ever ask you who you were?

Knock, knock.
Who's there?
Catsup.
Catsup who?
Catsup in the tree.

Knock, knock.
Who's there?
Cargo.
Cargo who?
Cargo beep.

Knock, knock.
Who's there?
Thistle.
Thistle who?
Thistle be the last knock knock.

Knock, knock.
Who's there?
Major.
Major who?
Major answer the door, didn't I?

Knock, knock.
Who's there?
Artichokes.
Artichokes who?
Artichokes when he eats too fast.

Brushing With the Law

SPORTS CAR DRIVER: But I wasn't doing one hundred.
POLICE OFFICER: Maybe not. But I want to give you this ticket as first prize.

POLICEMAN: Miss, you were doing one hundred miles an hour back there.
GIRL: Isn't that great? And I just learned to drive yesterday.

A hippie in a car was going down a one-way street the wrong way. A policeman on a motorcycle drove up to him and asked: "Didn't you see that arrow back there?"
"Arrow?" exclaimed the hippie. "Man, I never saw the Indian."

POLICEMAN: Do you know anything about traffic laws?
WOMAN DRIVER: A little. What do you want to know?

PRISONER: The judge sent me here for the rest of my life.
GUARD: Got any complaints?
PRISONER: Do you call breaking rocks with a hammer REST?

A man was going down a one-way street the wrong way.
POLICE OFFICER: Do you know where you are going?
MAN: Yes. But I must be late. Everyone is coming back.

A woman was stalled at a corner as the traffic light kept changing. Yellow, red, green—yellow, red, green.

A policeman stepped over to her car and asked, "What's the matter, lady, don't we have any colors you like?"

LAWYER: You say you were about thirty-five feet from the accident? Now, please tell the court how far you can see clearly.
WITNESS: Well, I can see the sun, and they tell me it's about ninety-three million miles away.

JUDGE: The jury has found you innocent of the charge of stealing.
DEFENDANT: Does that mean I can keep the watch?

POLICE OFFICER: What's the idea of racing through town at eighty miles an hour?
MOTORIST: I don't have any brakes and I want to get home before something happens.

GIRL: My dad can hold up an automobile with one hand.
BOY: Gee, he must be pretty strong.
GIRL: No, he's a policeman.

POLICEMAN: Didn't you see that thirty-mile-per-hour sign?

DRIVER: No, Officer. I was going too fast to see it.

The new convict walked into his prison cell. "How long is your sentence?" asked the old occupant.

"Twelve years."

"Mine is twenty," said the old con. "You get out first, so take the bed near the door."

BURGLAR: The police are coming. Quick, jump out the window.

ACCOMPLICE: But we're on the thirteenth floor.

BURGLAR: Do as I say. This is no time to be superstitious.

POLICEMAN: I've had my eyes on you for some time, miss.

GIRL: Fancy that. I thought you were arresting me for speeding.

Young lady driver presenting parking ticket to policeman: "Did you lose this? I found it on my windshield."

MAN: Have you seen a policeman around here?

BOY: I'm sorry. I haven't seen one all day.
MAN: Well then, stick 'em up.

TRAFFIC OFFICER: When I saw you driving down the road, I said to myself, "Sixty-five at least."
LADY DRIVER: Well, you're wrong. It's only my hat that makes me look older.

With a grinding of brakes, the officer pulled up his squad car and shouted to a little boy playing in the field: "Say, sonny, have you seen an airplane coming down anywhere around here?"

"No, sir," replied the boy, trying to hide his slingshot. "I've been shooting at the bottle on the fence."

A young teen-ager was dragged into court for a traffic violation.

"You see, Judge," said the teen-ager. "I didn't want to turn but the sign said: 'No. U turn.'"

JUDGE: Why did you park your car there?
DRIVER: The sign said, "Fine for Parking."

PRISON WARDEN (to prisoners): Next week is my tenth anniversary as warden of this prison. What shall we do to celebrate?
PRISONER: Have an open house.

JUDGE (to convicted prisoner): Thirty dollars or thirty days.
PRISONER: I'll take the thirty dollars. I need the money.

MOTORIST: Was I driving too fast?
POLICEMAN: Not at all. You were flying too low.

JUDGE: Have you been up before me previously?
PRISONER: I don't know. What time do you get up?

ZACK: What's the matter with your face?
MACK: Had a bit of an argument with some guy.
ZACK: Why didn't you call a cop?
MACK: Didn't have to. He was one.

POLICEMAN: You were going over sixty miles an hour.
MOTORIST: Imagine that, a twenty-mile-an-hour tail wind!

Then there was the mixed-up bank robber who shoved several hundred dollar bills into the teller's cage and said, "Quick, empty all the brown paper bags out of your drawer."

What do you get when you take the engine from a Ford, the wheels from a Cadillac, and the transmission from a Chevrolet?

ANSWER: Charged with larceny.

A man reported that his car had been "stripped." "They took the steering wheel, clutch pedal, dashboard, brake pedal, accelerator pedal, and radio," he complained.

The police said they would investigate.

A little while later, the man called the police again. "Forget about that theft report," he said. "I was sitting in the back seat."

A man was found walking along the street with a desk strapped to his back, a typewriter dangling from one arm, and a copying machine dangling from the other arm. He was arrested for impersonating an office.

A young lawyer looking for a place to establish a practice asked a local real estate salesperson, "Do you have a criminal lawyer in this town?"

"We certainly do," answered the realtor, "but we haven't been able to pin anything on him yet."

Two men robbed a farmhouse. There was no one around except cows, pigs, and chickens at the time of the robbery. Nevertheless the sheriff arrested the thieves less than an hour after the robbery.

"How did you know?" asked a friend of the sheriff.

"Don't you know someone always squeals?" answered the sheriff.

JUDGE: Do you know that you are here for drinking too much?
DEFENDANT: Great. Let's get started!

A man was going down a one-way street the wrong way. When an officer said, "This is a one-way street," the man said, "I'm only going one way."

DETECTIVE: So the prisoner got away. Did you guard all the exits?
POLICEMAN: Yes. But he must have slipped out through one of the entrances.

DRIVER: What's the problem, officer?
POLICEMAN: You were going seventy miles an hour.
DRIVER: You must be mistaken, I've only been driving fifteen minutes.

JUDGE: Give your name, occupation, and the charge against you.

PRISONER: My name is Spark. I'm an electrician. And the charge is battery.

JUDGE (to jailer): Alright. Put him in a dry cell.

PRISONER: This is a terrible shock.

Healthy Jokes

PATIENT: Doctor, do you think cranberries are healthy?
DOCTOR: Well, I've never heard one complain.

Five-year-old Susy was facing a minor surgical operation, and her mother told her: "Be a brave little girl, and Mama will get you a nice kitten."

Mother was sitting close by when Susy came out of the ether. She leaned forward to catch the youngster's first words.

The child opened her eyes, grimaced weakly, and muttered: "What a bum way to get a cat!"

The man went to the doctor and complained that his eyes bulged, his head ached, his ears were ringing, and he had trouble breathing. The man was sent to the hospital and had many tests, but the doctors could not diagnose his illness.

After the man left the hospital he went to buy some shirts to cheer himself up.

"What size?" asked the clerk.

"Fifteen neck, thirty-two sleeve."

"Sir," answered the salesman, "just looking at you I can see you are a seventeen neck."

"But I've always worn a size fifteen."

"You keep wearing size fifteen," said the salesman, "and your eyes will bulge, your head ache, your ears will ring, and you will have trouble breathing."

After a thorough physical examination, the doctor eyed his tall, very thin patient.

"Well, doc," said the patient, "how do I stand?"

"Son," said the doctor, "I don't know. I think it's a miracle."

LUNG SPECIALIST: It is my considered opinion that a man who sings at the top of his voice for an hour each day will never be troubled by chest complaints in his old age.

MEDICAL STUDENT: He probably won't even be troubled by old age.

DOCTOR: What was that tightwad patient complaining about now?

NURSE: He says he got well before all the medicine was used up.

CONNIE: Did you feel better after you went to the dentist?

LYLE: I certainly did. He wasn't in.

We've made great medical progress in the last generation. What used to be merely an itch is now an allergy.

"There's nothing wrong with you," said the psychiatrist to his patient. "Why, you're as sane as I am."

"But, Doctor!" said the patient as he brushed wildly at himself. "It's the butterflies! They're all over me."

"For heaven's sake," cried the doctor. "Don't brush them off on me."

An old man was having trouble with the sight in his left eye, so he went to a doctor. The doctor gave him a thorough examination and said, "There is nothing wrong with your eye. Its dimming sight is caused by old age."

The old man replied, "Nonsense and poppycock. The right eye is the same age as the left and I see fine with it."

"Doctor," asked the patient anxiously, "if I let you operate on me, can you promise that I'll be back playing the piano in a week or two?"

"Well, I can't promise the piano," returned the doctor cheerfully, "but the last patient on whom I performed this operation was playing a harp within twenty-four hours."

An eminent surgeon had an aversion to being called "doctor." Plain "mister" was all he wanted to be. Or to his friends, "Joe."

He was playing golf one morning when an acquaintance on the next fairway shouted cheerily, "Good morning there, Doctor."

The surgeon shouted back gruffly, "Good

morning to you, manufacturer of shirts, underwear, and fancy pajamas."

DOCTOR: Is there any insanity in your family?
STUDENT: There must be. They keep writing me for money.

Two radiologists were examining an X-ray photograph.
"Good photo," said one.
"Fairly good, but it flatters the left lung," said the other.

"Why did you tear out the back part of that new book?" asked the doctor's wife.
"Sorry, dear," said the absentminded surgeon. "The part you speak of was labeled 'Appendix' and I took it out without thinking."

PATIENT: That bill of yours was highway robbery. It made my blood boil.
DOCTOR: That will be thirty-five dollars more for sterilizing your system.

YOUNG DOCTOR: Well, Dad, now that I've just become a doctor, can you give me some rules for success?
FATHER: Always write your prescriptions illegibly and your bills very plainly.

A medical student who prescribed an overdose on one of his written examinations went to see his professor shortly afterwards in order to change his answer. The professor had already graded the paper and said, "It's too late. The patient has died."

The psychiatrist was testing the mentality of his patient. "Do you ever hear voices without being able to tell who is speaking, or where the voices are coming from?" he asked.
"Yes, sir," the patient replied.
"And when does this occur?" questioned the doctor.
"When I answer the telephone."

The instructor at the medical college exhibited a diagram.
"The subject here limps," he explained, "because one leg is shorter than the other." He then turned to one of the students. "Now," he said, "what would you do in such a case?"
The student pondered earnestly for a moment. "Well," he announced finally, "I think that under the circumstances, I would limp, too."

The weary surgeon took one last look at his work. The patient was fixed up: two arms set, four stitches over one eye, a plaster cast on one leg, and a small inset in the skull. The patient motioned to him and said, "Say, doc, I don't know just when I'm going to be able to pay you for all this. I've got a few hundred dollars saved up in the bank, but to tell you the truth, I'm saving that for an emergency."

OPHTHALMOLOGIST: Is there any letter on the chart that you can't read?
PATIENT: What chart?

PATIENT: I feel funny, Doctor. What shall I do?
DOCTOR: Go on television.

HORACE: Harry, is it true that an apple a day will keep the doctor away?
HARRY: Yes. Why?
HORACE: Well, I kept ten doctors away this morning, but I think I'd like to see one this afternoon.

A man visited a psychiatrist because he thought that he was a canary. A few months later, his wife phoned the doctor to inquire how her husband was progressing.

"Fine," came the reply. "Lady, I haven't heard a peep out of him."

PATIENT: Doctor, I can't get my sleep at night. I keep having the same dream about a door with a sign. I push and push, but I never can get it open.
DOCTOR: What does the sign say?
PATIENT: "Pull!"

PATIENT: Will I be able to read when I get my glasses?
DOCTOR: Indeed you will.
PATIENT: Well, that's fine. I never knew how before.

DOCTOR: Are you taking care of your cold?
PATIENT: I've had it a week, and it's as good as new.

DOCTOR: Is there any insanity in your family?
HOUSEWIFE: Just my husband. He thinks he's boss.

A little boy went to the dentist to have a tooth pulled. Seeing that the boy was frightened, the dentist gave him a tranquilizer.
"Feel braver now?" the dentist asked.
"You said it," the boy replied. "I'd like to see anybody try to yank my tooth out now."

"Did you say the man was shot in the woods, Doctor?"
"No. I said he was shot in the lumbar region."

DOCTOR: Have you had your iron today?
PATIENT: Well, I've been biting my nails.

DOCTOR: Have you ever had trouble with appendicitis?
PATIENT: Only when I try to spell it.

DOCTOR: What are you taking for that cold?
PATIENT: I don't know. Make me an offer.

DOCTOR: You will have to stop worrying and thinking about yourself so much. Throw yourself into your work.
PATIENT: But, Doctor, I run a cement mixer.

FIRST MAN: My doctor tells me I can't play golf.
SECOND MAN: He's played with you too, huh?

A man went to a doctor because he had a stiff neck. The doctor told him to put cold towels on it. He did what the doctor said and the stiff neck got worse. The man's maid then told him to put hot towels on his neck and the stiff neck got better. When the man visited the doctor again he told him what had happened.

"That's funny," said the doctor. "My maid said to use cold towels."

MINDY: Did you hear about the tongue-tied rabbit who went to the dentist to get his tooth extracted?
CRAIG: No.
MINDY: The dentist asked if he wanted gas, and the rabbit said, "No. I'm an ether bunny."

A doctor was walking along one day when he fell into a farmer's well. The farmer came over and told the doctor to take care of the sick and leave the well alone.

DOCTOR (to woman complaining about his bill): Don't forget this. I made eight house calls when Edward had the chicken pox.
WOMAN: And don't forget this. He infected the whole school for you.

DOCTOR: The check you gave me came back.
PATIENT: So did the pain in my chest.

PATIENT: Doctor, I'm a grown man, but I still have a childish fear of thunder. Can you help me to overcome it?
DOCTOR: Why, of course. Just do as I do when it thunders. Put your head under the pillow and it will go away.

DOCTOR: OK, now stick out your tongue.
PATIENT: What for? I'm not mad at you.

PATIENT: Well, doc, you certainly kept your promise when you said that you'd have me walking again in a month.
DOCTOR: Good. I'm glad to hear it.
PATIENT: Yes. I had to sell my car when I got your bill.

MOTHER: What are you jumping up and down for?
SON: I took my medicine and forgot to shake the bottle.

PATIENT: What shall I do? I have water on the knee.
DOCTOR: Wear pumps.

The doctor's twelve-year-old son and his playmate discovered a skeleton in a closet in the doctor's office.

"Who's that?" asked the playmate.

"Oh, that," answered the doctor's son, "that's Dad's first patient."

PATIENT: Doctor, I seem to be on pins and needles.
DOCTOR: Stand up. You're sitting on my nurse's pincushion.

A doctor had an urgent call from a man saying that his small son had swallowed a fountain pen.

"I'll be there right away," said the doctor, "but what are you doing in the meantime?"

The man replied, "Using a pencil."

PATIENT: Doc, how can I avoid falling hair?
DOCTOR: Jump out of the way.

PATIENT: Doc, after the operation on my hands, will I be able to play the piano?
DOCTOR: Of course.
PATIENT: That's wonderful. I've never been able to play the piano before.

PATIENT: Doctor, I'm frightened to death.
DOCTOR: I know just how you feel. You are my first patient.

MARY: The doctor told me to drink some lemonade after a hot bath.
JANE: Did you drink the lemonade?
MARY: No. I haven't finished drinking the hot bath yet.

DOCTOR: Please face this window. Now stick out your tongue.
PATIENT: Why do I have to face the window?
DOCTOR: I don't like my neighbor.

A surgeon was completing his two-thousandth operation. Another doctor walked in and asked, "How did you accomplish such a remarkable feat?"

The surgeon replied: "It took a lot of patients."

PATIENT: Oh, doc. I've got a headache, a stomachache, my back hurts, and my eyes itch.
DOCTOR: You sound like a television commercial.

JOAN: It's predicted that in ten years, poison ivy will be unknown.
JAMES: What a rash prediction.

DOCTOR: Are you taking that cough medicine that I gave you?
PATIENT: After I tasted it, I decided that I would rather cough.

A certain doctor claims that he can cure a woman of just about any complaint that she has simply by telling her that it's a sign of old age.

DENTIST: Stop making faces. I haven't touched your tooth yet.
PATIENT: I know you haven't, but you're standing on my foot.

A young student spent his summers working in a butcher shop in the daytime and working as an orderly in a hospital at night. One evening, he was instructed to wheel a patient on a stretcher into surgery. The patient, a very frightened lady, looked up at the student and let out an unearthly scream. "My goodness," she wailed, "it's my butcher."

Health hint: Brush your teeth regularly with an electric toothbrush and see your electrician twice a year.

DOCTOR: Have you carried out my instructions?
PATIENT: All but one. I can't take that two-mile walk every morning that you advised. I get all wet.
DOCTOR: I don't understand.
PATIENT: I forgot to tell you that I'm a lighthouse keeper.

An acupuncture specialist, annoyed by a late-night call from a patient, told the man, "Take two pins and call me in the morning."

DOCTOR: What was the most you ever weighed?
PATIENT: One hundred fifty-four pounds.

DOCTOR: What was the least you ever weighed?
PATIENT: Eight pounds.

DOCTOR: Your cough sounds better.
PATIENT: Thank you. I've been practicing all night.

PATIENT: Doctor, last night I dreamed I ate a marshmallow.
DOCTOR: What's so bad about that?
PATIENT: When I woke up, the pillow was gone.

PATIENT (on the telephone): Doctor, I have the strangest symptoms. My head feels squeezed, I smell something peculiar, my voice sounds strange, and one foot is cold. What could be the matter?
DOCTOR: You probably have one sock pulled over your head.

OLD FRIEND: What are you doing with yourself now?
STUDENT: I'm in college taking medicine.
OLD FRIEND: I'm sorry. How do you feel now?

PATIENT: Doctor, I just swallowed a harmonica. What should I do?

DOCTOR: I'll be right over. Meanwhile, keep calm and be happy.
PATIENT: Happy about what?
DOCTOR: That you weren't playing the piano.

DOCTOR (examining a middle-aged man): Most of my younger patients have thirty-two-inch waists. You have a generation gap of about thirteen inches.

PATIENT: Doctor, I think I have amnesia.
DOCTOR: How long have you had it?
PATIENT: Had what?

PATIENT: You've pulled every tooth but the right one.
DENTIST: I'm getting to it. I'm getting to it.

DOCTOR: What's the condition of the boy who swallowed the half-dollar?
NURSE: No change yet.

PATIENT: Doctor, why do you whistle when you operate?
DOCTOR: It helps to keep my mind off my work.

BARBARA: Did you hear about the surgeon who became a comedian?
MARTY: Yes. He has his patients in stitches.

PATIENT: Doctor, every time I drink coffee, I get a pain in my eye.
DOCTOR: Take the spoon out of the cup before you drink the coffee.

DOCTOR: Did you go to another doctor before you came to see me?
PATIENT: No. I went to a drugstore.
DOCTOR: What foolish thing did the pharmacist tell you?
PATIENT: He told me to come to you.

DOCTOR: I'm sorry to have to tell you your wife's mind is completely gone.
HUSBAND: I'm not surprised. She's been giving me a piece of it for twenty-five years.

PATIENT: Doctor, help me. My neck feels like a pipe, my head feels like a piece of iron, and my muscles feel like steel bands!
DOCTOR: Don't call me. Call the plumber.

A man reading a newspaper turned to his wife and said, "According to the statistics in this article, every time I breathe someone dies."
His wife replied, "Would you mind breathing the other way?"

DOCTOR: How is your wife coming along on her reducing diet?

HUSBAND: Just fine, she disappeared yesterday.

PATIENT: How can I cure myself of snoring?
DOCTOR: Try sleeping in the other room.

The doctor drove up to the farm to deliver the family's tenth child. As he turned into the driveway, he almost hit a duck. When the father opened the door to let him in the doctor said, "You know, I almost ran over your duck."
"That was no duck," said the father, "that was the stork with its legs worn down."

DOCTOR: Your right leg will be a little swollen, but I wouldn't worry about it.
PATIENT: If your leg was swollen I wouldn't worry about it either.

MEDICAL SCHOOL PROFESSOR: Why did you freeze the Band-Aids?
MEDICAL STUDENT: They're for cold cuts.

The patient was giving the doctor a difficult time, talking when the doctor was using the stethoscope, refusing to say "ah," and being unco-operative in every possible way.
"Please," said the exasperated doctor, "I'm losing my patience."

"I shouldn't be here either," answered the patient.

WORRIED PATIENT: But, Doctor, fifty per cent of people who have this operation die.
DOCTOR: Don't worry, I've already lost more than my fifty per cent.

A tightwad visited a dentist to have his tooth pulled, but hesitated when he heard about the cost. "Forty dollars is an awful lot of money for about five minutes' work," he said.
"Well, if you'd like," said the dentist, "I can pull it out slowly."

Riddles, Riddles, Riddles!

Who's fat, wear's a red suit, carries a big bag and falls down chimneys?
ANSWER: Santa Klutz.

What has a head and a foot but can't walk?
ANSWER: A bed.

Why don't ducks tell jokes while they are flying?
ANSWER: Because they would quack up.

What's pie in the sky?
ANSWER: A flying pizza.

What's the best year for a kangaroo?
ANSWER: Leap year.

What's white and goes up?
ANSWER: A confused snowflake.

What bird is a thief?
ANSWER: A robin.

Why did the man tell jokes to the mirror?
ANSWER: He wanted to see it crack up.

Why did the chicken cross the road?
ANSWER: To watch the man on the other side lay bricks.

What did the horse do when it swallowed a dollar?
ANSWER: It bucked.

What did one magnet say to the other magnet?
ANSWER: "I'm attracted to you."

Why did the man take his hammer to bed?
ANSWER: So he could hit the hay.

Why is a cup of coffee like an elevator?
ANSWER: They both give you a lift.

What gets answers but never asks questions?
ANSWER: A doorbell.

Why do lions eat raw meat?
ANSWER: Because they don't know how to cook.

What do polite lambs say to their mothers?
ANSWER: Thank ewe.

Why did the farmer feed money to his cow?
ANSWER: Because he wanted rich milk.

Why didn't Noah catch more fish when he was on the ark?
ANSWER: He only had two worms.

What would you get if you crossed a dog and a cat?
ANSWER: An animal that chased itself.

What is pointed in one direction and headed in the other?
ANSWER: A nail.

Why are the prairies so flat in the West?
ANSWER: Because the sun sets on them.

What does one car approaching a railroad crossing at eighty miles per hour, plus one train approaching the same railroad crossing at one hundred eight miles per hour equal?
ANSWER: A caboose full of scrap metal.

What is the noisiest part of a tree?
ANSWER: The bark.

If athletes get athlete's foot, what do astronauts get?
ANSWER: Missile toe.

What did one atom say to the other atom?
ANSWER: "Let's split up and charge the town."

What would happen if you ate yeast and polish?
ANSWER: You'd rise and shine.

What is the worst weather for rats and mice?
ANSWER: When it's raining cats and dogs.

Why does lightning shock people?
ANSWER: Because it doesn't know how to conduct itself.

Where does a jellyfish get its jelly?
ANSWER: From ocean currents.

Why was the pilot angry when the air controller told him to go to a higher altitude?
ANSWER: It made him soar.

What soap is the hardest?
ANSWER: Cast-steel.

What animal makes the closest approach to man?
ANSWER: The mosquito, if you don't swat it.

If there were five flies in the kitchen, which one would be the cowboy?
ANSWER: The one on the range.

What is the best way to prevent infection from biting insects?
ANSWER: Don't bite any.

If you had a shotgun and only one shell and a bull was chasing you, and you climbed a tree and found a copperhead snake there, which

would you shoot first, the bull or the copperhead?
ANSWER: The snake. You can shoot the bull any time.

Why did the man stand behind the mule?
ANSWER: He thought he'd get a kick out of it.

What would you call it if a sea gull flew out and landed on a channel marker?
ANSWER: Buoy meets gull.

What kind of a coat is it that has no buttons and is put on wet?
ANSWER: A coat of paint.

What would you get if you crossed a potato with an onion?
ANSWER: A potato with watery eyes.

Why were the Dark Ages called the Dark Ages?
ANSWER: Because they had so many knights.

What animal is satisfied with the least nourishment?
ANSWER: The moth. It eats nothing but holes.

What is a skeleton?
ANSWER: A person inside out with his outside off.

Why was the train conductor killed and the passenger was not when they both touched the third rail?
ANSWER: The passenger was a non-conductor.

What is commonly called brain food?
ANSWER: Noodle soup.

What kind of sentence would you get if you broke the law of gravity?
ANSWER: A suspended sentence.

Why do bees hum?
ANSWER: They don't know the words.

What did one herring say to the other herring?
ANSWER: Be thy brother's kipper.

Why is paper money more valuable than coins?
ANSWER: When you put a bill in your pocket, you double it. And when you take it out of your pocket, you find it in-creases.

What's the best way to send a wig from one place to another?
ANSWER: Hair mail.

What's the difference between a hill and a pill?
ANSWER: One gives you a hard time going up; the other gives you a hard time going down.

Why are all birds poor?
ANSWER: They all have bills.

Why are dogs affectionate children?
ANSWER: Because they lick their paws.

What kind of cane can make you move very fast?
ANSWER: A hurricane.

Why doesn't the ink spot on your shirt go away?
ANSWER: Because it's stain.

What is likely to be dirtier after taking a bath than before?
ANSWER: The bathtub.

What do pigs study in first-aid class?
ANSWER: Snout-to-snout resuscitation.

What's the difference between sunrise and sunset?
ANSWER: A day.

What has many tails but no head?
ANSWER: A collection of short stories.

Why did the man put the clock under his desk?
ANSWER: He wanted to work overtime.

Why can't the world come to an end?
ANSWER: Because it is round.

What's the quietest bee?
ANSWER: A mumble bee.

Why did the girl wash the rabbit?
ANSWER: Because her mother told her her hare was dirty.

Who does the rabbit in love dream of?
ANSWER: He dreams of Jeanie; she's a light brown hare.

What do you do when you wash a chicken?
ANSWER: Give a henna rinse.

What moves faster—hot or cold?
ANSWER: Hot. Everybody can catch cold.

What has twenty heads and gets hot if rubbed the right or wrong way?
ANSWER: A book of matches.

Why does a monkey scratch himself?
ANSWER: Because he's the only one who knows where it itches.

What time is it when you sit on a tack?
ANSWER: Spring time.

What is a three-season bed?
ANSWER: One without a spring.

What did one ear say to the other?
ANSWER: "I didn't know we lived on the same block."

What lives in the winter, dies in the summer, and grows with its roots upward?
ANSWER: An icicle.

What did one candle say to the other?
ANSWER: "Going out tonight?"

What is a person who drinks too much hot chocolate?
ANSWER: A cocoanut.

What has its heart in its head?
ANSWER: Lettuce.

Where does a polar bear keep its money?
ANSWER: In a snow bank.

Why did the cow cross the road?
ANSWER: Because it was the chicken's day off.

What happens to the air conditioner when you pull its plug?
ANSWER: It loses its cool.

Why are oysters lazy?
ANSWER: Because they are always found in their bed.

When are vegetables like music?
ANSWER: When there are two beets to a measure.

What do twelve apples and twelve bananas equal?
ANSWER: Twenty-four banapples.

What is similar about a blotter and a lazy dog?
ANSWER: A blotter is an ink-lined plane, an inclined plane is a slope up, a slow pup is a lazy dog.

What is the best thing to put on a pie?
ANSWER: Your teeth.

What did the three-hundred-pound mouse say?
ANSWER: "Here, kitty, kitty."

If I see a field full of cows, how can I count them quickly?
ANSWER: Count their hooves and divide by four.

What did the acorn say when he grew up?
ANSWER: Geometry.

What causes trees to become petrified?
ANSWER: The wind makes them rock.

Why couldn't the pony talk?
ANSWER: He was a little horse.

What's higher than a house and seems smaller than a mouse?
ANSWER: A star.

What did one flea say to the other while they were standing on a street corner?
ANSWER: "I'm taking a greyhound to Main Street."

If a baby camel were born with a straight back, what would his mother call him?
ANSWER: Hump-free.

What has three eyes and three noses?
ANSWER: A vote that is tied.

What did the little dolphin say when he bumped into the bully dolphin?
ANSWER: "I didn't do it on porpoise."

What is the highest form of animal life?
ANSWER: The giraffe.

On which side does a chicken have the most feathers?
ANSWER: On the outside.

What did one volcano say to the other volcano?
ANSWER: "Lava, come back to me."

What bus crossed the ocean?
ANSWER: Columbus.

Why should fish be well educated?
ANSWER: They are found in schools.

Who is Snow White's best friend?
ANSWER: Egg White. The yolk's on you.

If buttercups are yellow, what color are hiccups?
ANSWER: Burple.

What does a marine become after he dives under water?
ANSWER: A submarine.

What kind of leather makes the best shoes?
ANSWER: I don't know, but banana peels make the best slippers.

What would happen if you swallowed some uranium?
ANSWER: You'd get atomic ache.

How can Batman tell when it's spring?
ANSWER: When Robin starts laying eggs.

What is bought by the yard, but worn by the foot?
ANSWER: A carpet.

What part of the car causes the most accidents?
ANSWER: The nut that holds the wheel.

How was spaghetti invented?
ANSWER: Some fellow used his noodle.

What word begins with an *E* and ends with an *E* and only has one letter in it?
ANSWER: Envelope.

What fruit is on a dime?
ANSWER: A date.

Why is the barn so noisy?
ANSWER: The cows have horns.

How do you communicate with a fish?
ANSWER: Drop him a line.

What kind of bird is in your throat?
ANSWER: A swallow.

Why does a hen lay eggs?
ANSWER: Because if she dropped them they would break.

What has four wheels and flies?
ANSWER: A garbage truck.

What do they do with leftover doughnut holes?
ANSWER: They tie them together with string and make fish nets.

Mr. Portman was a butcher. He was six feet tall and wore size twelve shoes. What did he weigh?
ANSWER: Meat.

Why did the little girl punch her pillow every night?
ANSWER: Because she heard her mother say, "I'm asleep as soon as I hit the pillow."

How many balls of twine would it take to reach the moon?
ANSWER: Only one, if it were long enough.

Can you spell something that has over one hundred letters in it?
ANSWER: Post Office.

What did Tarzan say when he was tired of butter?
ANSWER: "Oh, Leo."

Why does time fly?
ANSWER: Because so many people are trying to kill it.

Why did the letter arrive wet?
ANSWER: Because of the postage dew.

What did one magnet say to the other magnet?
ANSWER: "You're very attractive today."

What pine has the longest and sharpest needles?
ANSWER: A porcupine.

Why is your heart like a policeman?
ANSWER: Because it follows a regular beat.

What is the best way to keep a fish from smelling?
ANSWER: Cut off its nose.

What is the best way to find a pin?
ANSWER: Walk around in your bare feet.

What did one road say to the other road?
ANSWER: "Do you have that run-down feeling?"

What is brought to the table and cut but never eaten?
ANSWER: A deck of cards.

Why should you not tell pigs secrets?
ANSWER: Because they are squealers.

What gets wetter the more it dries?
ANSWER: A towel.

Why do chickens get their mouths washed out with soap?
ANSWER: Because they use fowl language.

What is an alligator when it is sick?
ANSWER: An illigator.

What do you do for a drowning rat?
ANSWER: Mouse-to-mouse resuscitation.

What is the hitchhiker's tax?
ANSWER: Thumb tax.

What do you call the great leopard hunter?
ANSWER: The spot remover.

If you went hunting and saw a tiger and a lion, which would you shoot first?
ANSWER: The gun.

Why do they have mirrors on candy machines?
ANSWER: So you can see your face when the candy doesn't come out.

What did one duck say to the other?
ANSWER: "No wise quacks."

What did the old woman who lived in the shoe ever do with all her children?
ANSWER: She sent them to boot camp.

What did the cannibal say when he had a stomachache?
ANSWER: "It must have been someone I ate."

What did the midgets sail the ocean on?
ANSWER: Shrimp boats.

What did the doctors sail the ocean on?
ANSWER: Blood vessels.

What smells the most in a bakery?
ANSWER: Your nose.

What did the baby porcupine say when he backed into a cactus?
ANSWER: "Is that you, Mama?"

Why do ducks fly South for the winter?
ANSWER: Because it's too far to walk.

What did the muffler say to the bumper?
ANSWER: "Boy am I exhausted."

What did the big flower say to the little flower?
ANSWER: "Hi, Bud."

What would you get if you crossed a quarter-pounder with a bee?
ANSWER: A humburger.

What animal do you look like when you take a bath?
ANSWER: A little bear.

What satellite was never launched?
ANSWER: The moon.

When is a boat like snow?
ANSWER: When it is adrift.

Why should you never touch a perfect circle?
ANSWER: Because it's three hundred sixty degrees.

What Roman numeral grows?
ANSWER: IV (ivy).

What's a compact dog house?
ANSWER: A pup tent.

When does a bed grow longer?
ANSWER: At night, when two feet are added to it.

What kind of flowers can you find in a zoo?
ANSWER: Dandy lions and tiger lilies.

Why is cheese considered to be an artist?
ANSWER: Because it draws mice.

Why is a calendar so sad?
ANSWER: Because its days are numbered.

What color is the longest lasting?
ANSWER: Evergreen.

What is the best way to catch a fish?
ANSWER: Have someone throw it to you.

Where is the only place on a beach that doesn't have litter?
ANSWER: The trash can.

What man never does a day's work in his lifetime?
ANSWER: A night watchman.

What is the best way to keep a skunk from smelling?
ANSWER: Hold his nose.

What is in an astronaut's sandwich?
ANSWER: Launchmeat.

When do the leaves begin to turn?
ANSWER: Right before examinations.

What do you get when you cross a banana with a knife?
ANSWER: A banana split.

If you crossed Ferdinand the Brahman bull with Illizer the Jersey cow, what would the offspring be called?
ANSWER: Ferdilizer.

Who did Cal Ifornia and Ken Tuckee take on their dates?
ANSWER: Miss Ouri and Miss Issippi.

What happens to a duck when he flies upside down?
ANSWER: He quacks up.

What did one fly say to the other fly?
ANSWER: "I just passed my screen test."

What has a mouth and doesn't talk, and a bed that it doesn't sleep in?
ANSWER: A river.

Could you light a candle if you had a box of candles and no matches?
ANSWER: Yes. Just take a candle out of the box and you will make the box a candle lighter.

What kind of a sheet can't be used on a bed?
ANSWER: A sheet of ice.

Why did the jelly roll?
ANSWER: It saw the apple turnover.

What does a hippie frog say?
ANSWER: "Dig it. Dig it."

What did one mountain say to another after an earthquake?
ANSWER: "It wasn't my fault."

What is the first problem that a golfer's son learns?
ANSWER: Two plus two equals fore.

Why is a dog man's best friend?
ANSWER: He wags his tail instead of his tongue.

What kind of animals can jump higher than a house?
ANSWER: All kinds of animals. Houses can't jump.

What was the name of the very first fruit?
ANSWER: Adam's apple.

Why does a clock run?
ANSWER: Because it has ticks.

Why is a watch like a river?
ANSWER: Because it doesn't run long without winding.

Why is a half-moon heavier than a full moon?
ANSWER: A full moon is lighter.

Why does Snoopy want to quit the comic strips?
ANSWER: He's tired of working for Peanuts.

Why is that toothbrush in your coat lapel?
ANSWER: It's my class pin. I go to Colgate.

Why is two plus two equals five like your left foot?
ANSWER: Because it's not right.

What did the Beatles say when they saw an avalanche?
ANSWER: "Here come the Rolling Stones."

When is the best time to get a bite?
ANSWER: When you are fishing.

What is round at both ends and high in the middle?
ANSWER: Ohio.

Why did the man throw the clock out of the window?
ANSWER: He wanted to see time fly.

Why did the man shoot the clock?
ANSWER: He wanted to kill some time.

What flowers do women wear on their feet?
ANSWER: Lady's slippers.

If an egg came floating down the Ohio River, where would it have come from?
ANSWER: A hen.

Which is the left side of an apple pie?
ANSWER: The part that's not eaten.

What did the light bulb say to his girl friend?
ANSWER: "You really turn me on."

Why did the golfer wear two pair of pants?
ANSWER: In case he made a hole in one.

What ten-letter word starts with gas?
ANSWER: Automobile.

Why is your hand like a hardware store?
ANSWER: Because it has nails.

How do you play ticktacktoe?
ANSWER: Take a tick and tack it on your toe.

What do you get when you cross an owl with a goat?
ANSWER: A hootenanny.

What do you get when you cross a lion with a parrot?
ANSWER: I don't know, but you had better listen when it talks.

What is the center of gravity?
ANSWER: The letter V.

What is a carton full of ducks?
ANSWER: A box of quackers.

What would happen if all the cars in the United States were painted pink?
ANSWER: We would be a pink car nation.

Why is tennis a noisy game?
ANSWER: Each player raises a racket.

What is the difference between a cat and a comma?
ANSWER: A cat has claws at the end of its paws, and a comma has a pause at the end of its clause.

What time is it when the clock strikes thirteen?
ANSWER: Time to get it fixed.

What flowers are like a part of your face?
ANSWER: Tulips.

What is small, has four wheels, two headlights, and long hair?
ANSWER: A hippie driving a Volkswagen.

Why did Robin Hood rob the rich?
ANSWER: Because the poor had no money.

What did the balloon say to the pin?
ANSWER: "Hello, Buster."

What kind of bulbs should you never water?
ANSWER: Light bulbs.

What money can you pick up at the animal fair?
ANSWER: A bill from the duck, a greenback from the frog, a cent from the skunk, and four quarters from the cow.

What part of a fish weighs the most?
ANSWER: The scales.

What did the Beatles sing while they were sinking into the quicksand?
ANSWER: "I Want to Hold Your Hand."

What did Mrs. Paul Revere say to her husband?
ANSWER: "I don't care who's coming tonight, it's my turn to use the horse."

Why did the man drive his truck over the cliff?
ANSWER: He wanted to test his air brakes.

Why did the man put roller skates on his rocking chair?
ANSWER: He wanted to rock and roll.

Why did the chicken cross the road?
ANSWER: To get away from Colonel Sanders.

What has four feet, is gray, and has a trunk?
ANSWER: A mouse going on vacation.

What breaks but does not fall, and what falls but does not break?
ANSWER: Day breaks and night falls.

If one man has two sacks of flour, and another man has three sacks, which man has the lighter load?
ANSWER: The man with three has nothing but sacks.

Why did the man carry a bowl and spoon to the movies?
ANSWER: He heard that they were going to show a new serial.

Where are you when you are flying from New Zealand to Australia?
ANSWER: You're up over down under.

What's another name for a policeman's cookie?
ANSWER: A cop cake.

What goes snap, crackle, and pop?
ANSWER: A firefly with a short circuit.

When is a sailor like a plank?
ANSWER: When he boards a ship.

What has eight legs, six eyes, and feathers?
ANSWER: A man riding a horse and carrying a chicken.

What kind of candy bars are for girls only?
ANSWER: Hershey's.

What would you think if you found bones on the moon?
ANSWER: The cow didn't make it over.

What kind of flower would Lassie wear to a dance?
ANSWER: A cauliflower.

Why wasn't the cook in the kitchen?
ANSWER: Because the recipe said crack one egg and beat it.

What did one toe say to the other?
ANSWER: Don't look now, but there's a big heel following us.

What's the difference between the moon and the earth?
ANSWER: Space.

What do you call a broken record?
ANSWER: A smashed hit.

What animal drops from the clouds?
ANSWER: A rain deer.

What did the caveman say when he had a flat on his wooden wheel?
ANSWER: "I've got to get rid of those termites."

Why did the fly fly?
ANSWER: Because the spider spied her.

Why did the horse take a bale of hay to bed with him?
ANSWER: To feed the nightmare.

What is very hard to beat?
ANSWER: A hard-boiled egg.

What is the difference between a cloud and a boy getting a spanking?
ANSWER: The cloud pours rain and the boy roars pain.

If Ireland were to sink, what city would float?
ANSWER: Cork.

What did the man tell the coat?
ANSWER: "Straighten up if you want me to put you on."

What birds are always sad?
ANSWER: Bluebirds.

How would you start a lightning bug race?
ANSWER: On your mark, get set, glow!

What do cows do when they meet?
ANSWER: They have a milk shake.

Are bees good at arguments?
ANSWER: Yes. A bee always carries its point.

What do you call a bird that gets run over by a lawn mower?
ANSWER: Shredded tweets.

What happens when someone eats cookies before going to bed?
ANSWER: He has a crumby sleep.

What animal is on every legal document?
ANSWER: A seal.

What would you say if everyone in the United States sneezed at the same time?
ANSWER: "God Bless America."

Who would you hire to prepare a banquet on the moon?
ANSWER: A craterer.

How is a blackboard like a tally card?
ANSWER: You can chalk it up.

What's black and white and red all over?
ANSWER: A blushing penguin.

If a chicken and a half laid an egg and a half in a day and a half, how long would it take a rooster to sit on a doorknob and hatch a hardware store?
ANSWER: Give up? So did he.

In what month do girls talk the least?
ANSWER: February, because it's the shortest month.

What do you get if you cross a bed with a toaster?
ANSWER: A machine that pops people out of bed.

Why do Eskimos wash their clothes in Tide?
ANSWER: Because it's too cold to wash them out-tide.

What was the most fantastic feat of strength ever put on the map?
ANSWER: Wheeling West Virginia.

George Washington threw a dollar across the Rappahannock River; why can't we do this today?
ANSWER: Money doesn't go as far as it used to.

What did one side of the cell say to the other?
ANSWER: "Let's split."

What keeps a magazine alive?
ANSWER: Good circulation.

What was Adam and Eve's telephone number?
ANSWER: 281 apple.

What is so brittle that even to name it is to break it?
ANSWER: Silence.

What do you call it when one orange falls in love with another orange?
ANSWER: An orange crush.

Why do you go to bed at night?
ANSWER: Because the bed won't go to you.

What is six feet long, is green, and has eight eyes?
ANSWER: One of the Jolly Green Giant's sneakers.

How can you turn a pickle into another vegetable?
ANSWER: Throw it in the air and it comes down squash.

What's the difference between the North Pole and the South Pole?
ANSWER: All the difference in the world.

What did the plumber say to his assistant who was talking too much?
ANSWER: Pipe down.

What is the best way to prevent water from coming into the basement?
ANSWER: Don't pay the water bills.

What is white, gives milk, and has only one horn?
ANSWER: A milk truck.

A girl was locked in a room with only a piano in it. How did she open the door and get out in less than a minute?
ANSWER: She played the piano until she found the right key.

What animal never plays fair?
ANSWER: The cheetah.

What do you get when you put nitroglycerin in an eggshell?
ANSWER: An eggsplosive.

Why did the farmer put his cow on the scales?
ANSWER: He wanted to see the milk-he-weighed.

How is a chicken sitting on a fence post like a penny?
ANSWER: Head's on one side and tail's on the other.

Why would you expect a fisherman to be more honest than a shepherd?
ANSWER: A fisherman lives by hook and a shepherd lives by crook.

A man went to the woods on Wednesday, stayed a week, and came back on the same Wednesday. How did he do it?
ANSWER: His mule's name was Wednesday.

Why is the telephone company not going to have telephone poles any longer?
ANSWER: Because they are long enough.

Why is a ship the most polite thing in the world?
ANSWER: Because it always advances with a bow.

Which state has the smallest soft drinks?
ANSWER: Minnesota.

What did the canary say when its cage fell apart?
ANSWER: "Cheap, cheap."

What did Batman and Robin become when they were run over by a steamroller?
ANSWER: Flatman and Ribbon.

What is light and heavy, is little and makes big things?
ANSWER: An atom.

What does the constellation Orion, the Hunter, like best about the night sky?
ANSWER: Shooting stars.

Which side of the house does grass grow on?
ANSWER: The outside.

You are in a house with no electric current. In the kitchen are a coal stove, a kerosene lamp, and a candle. It is night, and you have only one match to light all three. Which should you light first?
ANSWER: The match.

What businessman drives his business away?
ANSWER: A taxi driver.

Why did the boy put the radio in the refrigerator?
ANSWER: He wanted to hear cool music.

What do you get when you cross a turtle with a porcupine?
ANSWER: A slowpoke.

What is orange and defends law and order?
ANSWER: The Lone Tangerine.

What did one pencil say to the other pencil?
ANSWER: "Write on."

What two musical keys should a man walking a tightrope think about?
ANSWER: C sharp or B flat.

Why are horses hard to get along with?
ANSWER: They always say, "Nay."

Why do college students call home collect?
ANSWER: They believe in free speech.

Why is the sea measured in knots?
ANSWER: To keep the ocean tide.

What kind of clothes did Cinderella wear?
ANSWER: Wish and wear.

What word is made shorter by adding two letters to it?
ANSWER: Short.

When is the weather worse than raining cats and dogs?
ANSWER: When it's hailing taxis.

When is your pocket empty but still has something in it?
ANSWER: When it has a hole in it.

What did the beaver say to the tree?
ANSWER: It's been nice gnawing you.

What happens when you make a long-distance call to Paris?
ANSWER: You get a French connection.

What do you call a rabbit with fleas?
ANSWER: Bugs Bunny.

What do you leave behind when you walk?
ANSWER: Your footsteps.

What's full of *T* and starts and ends with *T*?
ANSWER: A teapot.

What do you get when you cross a mink with a kangaroo?
ANSWER: A fur coat with pockets.

What do you call the process of recycling twice?
ANSWER: Bicycling.

What word is always pronounced wrong?
ANSWER: Wrong.

What did the astronaut see in his skillet?
ANSWER: An unidentified frying object.

What did Mars say to Saturn?
ANSWER: You have rings around your collar.

What's green and moves a lot?
ANSWER: A plant with the hiccups.

Why did the robber take a bath?
ANSWER: He wanted to make a clean getaway.

What would you get if you crossed an electric eel with a sponge?
ANSWER: Shock absorbers.

What seven letters do you say to a refrigerator with nothing in it?
ANSWER: *O I C U R M T.*

How do you make your hair dance?
ANSWER: Get a headband.

If a carrot and a cabbage race, who will win?
ANSWER: The cabbage wins because it is ahead.

What makes the Tower of Pisa lean?
ANSWER: It never eats.

What do you call a group of chemical elements?
ANSWER: The Atoms Family.

Why did the man put bug spray on his watch?
ANSWER: It had ticks.

What did the limestone say to the geologist?
ANSWER: "Don't take me for granite."

What did the first elevator say to the second elevator?
ANSWER: "I think I'm coming down with something."

What has eight legs and a quick draw?
ANSWER: Billy the Squid.

What did the mother and father lightning bug say about their baby son?
ANSWER: "He sure is bright."

How deep is a frog pond?
ANSWER: Kneedeep, kneedeep.

Why is a banana like a sweater?
ANSWER: You slip on both.

Why is a pencil like a riddle?
ANSWER: Because neither one is any good without a point.

Why did Mickey Mouse leave home?
ANSWER: He found out his father was a rat.

When is a person in a gaseous state?
ANSWER: When he is boiling mad.

What do you get when you cross one of the Beatles with a Rolling Stone?
ANSWER: A smashed bug.

How did the octopus go into battle?
ANSWER: Well armed.

What goes up but never comes down?
ANSWER: Your age.

What do you get when you cross a crab with a mathematician?
ANSWER: Snappy answers.

Why did the moon go to the bank?
ANSWER: To change quarters.

What's red, white, blue, and hairy?
ANSWER: Uncle Sam on his way to the barber shop.

What did one candle say to the other candle?
ANSWER: "Boy, these birthday parties really burn me up."

Who performs operations at the fish hospital?
ANSWER: The head sturgeon.

Why can't you tell secrets in the country?
ANSWER: Because the corn has ears, the potatoes have eyes, and beanstalk.

Why are snakes smart?
ANSWER: Because you can't pull their legs.

How did the bulldog get such a flat nose?
ANSWER: He was always chasing parked cars.

Where was Mickey Mouse when the lights went out?
ANSWER: In the dark.

What do you get when you cross a bird with a zero?
ANSWER: A flying none.

What is brown, has a hump, and lives at the North Pole?
ANSWER: A lost camel.

What kind of robber steals pigs?
ANSWER: A hamburglar.

What is a good way to keep a house warm?
ANSWER: Paint it with two coats.

What did the washcloth say to the dish towel?
ANSWER: "Meet me at the clothesline. That's where I hang out."

What has five fingers and no bones?
ANSWER: A glove.

How did the pig get from Texas to Florida?
ANSWER: The swine flu.

What has nothing left but a nose when it loses an eye?
ANSWER: Noise.

What made the pickle break up with his girl friend?
ANSWER: His feelings turned sour.

When is a clock dangerous?
ANSWER: When it strikes one.

Where does the sheep get his hair cut?
ANSWER: At the baa baa shop.

How do you make gold stew?
ANSWER: Add fourteen carrots.

Why is a crossword puzzle like a quarrel?
ANSWER: One word leads to another.

What did the glove say to the hand?
ANSWER: "I've got you covered."

What was the turtle doing on the freeway?
ANSWER: Two miles an hour.

When was beef the highest?
ANSWER: When the cow jumped over the moon.

If a rooster laid an egg, which way would the egg roll?
ANSWER: It wouldn't roll. Roosters don't lay eggs.

What gets wet as it dries?
ANSWER: A towel.

Which one of your schoolbooks is in trouble?
ANSWER: Your math book. It's filled with problems.

What two countries can you eat?
ANSWER: Turkey and Chile.

Why did Mickey Mouse go into space?
ANSWER: He wanted to find Pluto.

How do you drive a baby buggy?
ANSWER: Tickle his feet.

What three letters are robbers afraid of?
ANSWER: *I C U.*

What goes up and down and never touches the sky or ground?
ANSWER: A pump handle.

What happened to the two bedbugs who fell in love?
ANSWER: They got married in the spring.

What would you have if someone gave you a cow and two ducks?
ANSWER: Milk and quackers.

What did the apple say when he saw the peach coming?
ANSWER: "Here comes the fuzz."

What did the shrub say to the tree?
ANSWER: "Boy, I'm bushed."

What is smarter than a talking horse?
ANSWER: A spelling bee.

Why did the water bed go dry?
ANSWER: Because it didn't have any springs.

What did the man say to the clay pot?
ANSWER: "You're going to be fired."

Why is a dollar bill like a secret?
ANSWER: They are both hard to keep.

What did the workman say to the wall?
ANSWER: "One more crack and I'll plaster you."

What did the picture say to the wall?
ANSWER: "First, they framed me and then they hung me."

Why do ducks hang their heads?
ANSWER: To keep from quacking up.

Why is it so hard to talk with a goat around?
ANSWER: Because he always butts in.

Which star is the noisiest?
ANSWER: A shooting star.

What has twenty heads but can't think?
ANSWER: A book of matches.

What do you do when your toes fall off?
ANSWER: You call a toe truck.

What's a dog's favorite rock group?
ANSWER: The Rolling Bones.

What did the boy say as he looked out the window and the window fell down on him?
ANSWER: "That window is a pane in the neck."

What do you do when you have a loose tooth?
ANSWER: Use toothpaste.

What's gray and fights fires in the jungle?
ANSWER: Smokey the Elephant.

Why do dragons always sleep in the daytime?
ANSWER: Because they like to hunt knights.

What lies at the bottom of the ocean and shivers?
ANSWER: A nervous wreck.

What kind of bow is hard to tie?
ANSWER: A rainbow.

What's the difference between a jeweler and a jailer?
ANSWER: One sells watches, the other watches cells.

What did the chicken say when she laid the square egg?
ANSWER: Ouch.

What's the difference between an old penny and a new dime?
ANSWER: Nine cents.

How many feet are in a yard?
ANSWER: It depends on how many people are in the yard.

When can fifty people stand under an umbrella without getting wet?
ANSWER: When it's not raining.

What has neither weight nor width, length nor thickness, but can be measured accurately?
ANSWER: Time.

Why are farmers famous?
ANSWER: They are outstanding in their field.

What's more useful after it's broken?
ANSWER: An egg.

If a king sits on gold, who sits on silver?
ANSWER: The Lone Ranger.

What would you get if you crossed a four-leaf clover with poison ivy?
ANSWER: A rash of good luck.

What kind of horse runs only at night?
ANSWER: A nightmare.

What has holes in it but can hold water?
ANSWER: A sponge.

Why does Santa Claus have a garden?
ANSWER: Because he likes to Ho! Ho! Ho!

What did the leopard say after he finished lunch?
ANSWER: "Boy, that really hit the spot."

What happens if you tell a joke to a mirror?
ANSWER: It cracks up.

What is the best way to raise strawberries?
ANSWER: With a spoon.

What animal eats with his tail?
ANSWER: All of them, since they can't take off their tails to eat.

Why does the corn dislike the farmer?
ANSWER: Because he pulls the corn's ears.

What do you call a frightened skin diver?
ANSWER: Chicken of the Sea.

What is the laziest mountain on earth?
ANSWER: Mount Everest.

Why did the lady go outside with her purse open?
ANSWER: She expected some change in the weather.

What kind of birds should wear wigs?
ANSWER: Bald eagles.

Why can't you whisper in school?
ANSWER: It's not aloud.

What would you get if you put a swimming pool inside a movie house?
ANSWER: A dive-in movie.

Why is a flashlight like a piggy bank?
ANSWER: They're both smart. A flashlight is bright, a piggy bank has lots of sense.

What happens when a cat eats a lemon?
ANSWER: It turns into a sourpuss.

What is black and white with red all around?
ANSWER: A skunk in a red bathroom.

How would you address a six-foot karate expert?
ANSWER: Carefully and with great respect.

What would you yell at Donald to keep him from getting hit by a baseball?
ANSWER: Donald Duck.

Where does the snowman keep his money?
ANSWER: In the snow bank.

What goes on and on, has an *I* in the middle, and smells awful?
ANSWER: Onion.

What happens once in every minute, twice in every moment, and never in a thousand years?
ANSWER: The letter *M*.

Why did the orange stop in the middle of the road?
ANSWER: It ran out of juice.

What has two feet but can't walk?
ANSWER: A pair of socks.

Why is an empty purse always the same?
ANSWER: Because there is no change in it.

When is it bad luck to have a black cat following you?
ANSWER: When you are a mouse.

What do moose do at concerts?
ANSWER: Make moosic.

What can you hold without touching it?
ANSWER: Your tongue.

What is a wind?
ANSWER: Air in a hurry.

What's the difference between a train conductor and a teacher?
ANSWER: One minds the train and the other trains the mind.

What kind of nail does the carpenter try to avoid hitting?
ANSWER: A fingernail.

How quiet is a bowling alley?
ANSWER: Quiet enough to hear a pin drop.

When butchers have a dance, what is it called?
ANSWER: The meat ball.

What do you call a cow that is eating grass?
ANSWER: A lawn mooer.

What did George Washington say to his men just before he crossed the Delaware?
ANSWER: "Get into the boat, men."

When fish go to sleep, where do they go?
ANSWER: To the river bed.

What weighs the same no matter what size it is?
ANSWER: A hole.

What runs around all day and sleeps with its tongue out at night?
ANSWER: A shoe.

What kind of tree does everyone have on his hand?
ANSWER: A palm.

What's a flood?
ANSWER: A river that's too big for its bridges.

Why can't you tell a secret in the cornfield?
ANSWER: Because there are too many ears there.

What are Santa Claus's helpers called?
ANSWER: Subordinate clauses.

Why did the farmer name the pig ink?
ANSWER: Because it kept running out of the pen.

What do you call a monkey who sells potato chips?
ANSWER: A chipmunk.

What is unable to speak, unable to think, yet tells the truth when it's underfoot?
ANSWER: A scale.

What's the hardest thing about learning how to roller-skate?
ANSWER: The floor.

Why is a watermelon filled with water?
ANSWER: Because it's planted in the spring.

Why is the mailman a polluter?
ANSWER: He letters up the mailbox.

Why is an oyster like a smart person?
ANSWER: They both know when to keep their mouths shut.

What kind of shoes do lazy people wear?
ANSWER: Loafers.

What two things can't be eaten for breakfast?
ANSWER: Lunch and dinner.

Why does the dog wag its tail?
ANSWER: Because the tail can't wag the dog.

If two is company and three is a crowd, what are four and five?
ANSWER: Nine.

What did the bald man say when he got a comb for his birthday?
ANSWER: "I'll never part with it."

Why does a moth eat holes in the rug?
ANSWER: Because it wants to see the floor show.

What has no hands or feet but can still climb a fence?
ANSWER: A vine.

What is the most impolite dog?
ANSWER: A pointer.

What kind of a rock is green?
ANSWER: A shamrock.

Why is a bad boy like a melting ice cream cone?
ANSWER: They both need a good licking.

What is the fastest way to double your money?
ANSWER: Fold it in half.

Why is it cold at baseball games?
ANSWER: Because of all the fans.

What's so strange about the way a horse eats?
ANSWER: It eats best when it doesn't have a bit in its mouth.

What do bacteria have to do with arithmetic?
ANSWER: They multiply by dividing.

What runs all day, runs all night, but never gets anywhere?
ANSWER: A clock.

What can go around the world and still stay in one corner?
ANSWER: A postage stamp.

What kind of a dress can't be worn?
ANSWER: An address.

What's the difference between a fighter and a man with a cold?
ANSWER: One blows his nose and the other knows his blows.

How many people live in the world?
ANSWER: All of them.

Why is the Statue of Liberty's finger eleven inches long?
ANSWER: If it were one inch longer it would be a foot.

Why did the ballplayer bring rope to the game?
ANSWER: Because he wanted to tie the score.

Why does a cow wear a bell?
ANSWER: Because her horn doesn't work.

What did the man say when his dog ran away from home?
ANSWER: "Dog-gone."

When are eyes not eyes?
ANSWER: When the wind makes them water.

What never speaks unless it is spoken to, but can speak in every language?
ANSWER: An echo.

What vegetable's outside is thrown away so the inside can be cooked but the outside is eaten and the inside thrown away?
ANSWER: Corn.

What did one strawberry say to the other?
ANSWER: If you weren't so fresh, we wouldn't be in this jam.

Where were the first doughnuts fried?
ANSWER: In Greece.

Who does Batman's cooking?
ANSWER: Batty Crocker.

How are oranges and bells alike?
ANSWER: They both peal.

What happened when the boarding house blew up?
ANSWER: Roomers were flying.

What building has the most stories?
ANSWER: A library.

Why didn't the skeleton cross the road?
ANSWER: He didn't have the guts.

What's green and writes underwater?
ANSWER: A ball-point pickle.

What's a pipe cleaner?
ANSWER: A toothpick with long underwear.

Who was the first skin diver?
ANSWER: The mosquito.

Why is the sky all scratched up in the big city?
ANSWER: Because of the skyscrapers.

What is the beginning of eternity, the end of time and space, the beginning of every end, and the end of every place?
ANSWER: The letter *E*.

How do you know the pheasant is married?
ANSWER: Because of the ring around its neck.

Why is so little known about salivary glands?
ANSWER: Because they're so secretive.

Why did the boy drown in bed?
ANSWER: Because he fell into the spring after the bed spread and the pillow slipped.

What color would you paint the sun and the wind?
ANSWER: The sun rose and the wind blue.

What has eighteen legs and catches flies?
ANSWER: A baseball team.

Why were the Indians the first people in America?
ANSWER: They had reservations.

What goes through the woods without making a noise?
ANSWER: A path.

What is lighter than a feather, but a thousand men can't lift it?
ANSWER: Your shadow.

What's a pickle with a taillight?
ANSWER: A stuffed olive.

What happens to people who jaywalk?
ANSWER: They get that run-down feeling.

What can go up a chimney down, but not down a chimney up?
ANSWER: An umbrella.

Who is never hungry at Thanksgiving?
ANSWER: The turkey; it's always stuffed.

What inventions have helped people rise in the world?
ANSWER: Alarm clocks and elevators.

What did the pencil say to the sheet of paper?
ANSWER: "I dot my eyes on you."

What did the necktie say to the hat?
ANSWER: "You go on ahead, I'll hang around."

What's the difference between a deer being chased and a midget witch?
ANSWER: One is a hunted stag and the other is a stunted hag.

How do you know the ocean is a friendly place?
ANSWER: By its friendly waves.

Why did the boy put the ice in his aunt's bed?
ANSWER: He wanted to make his auntie freeze.

Why do hens lay eggs only in the daytime?
ANSWER: They become roosters at night.

What do they do with leftover doughnut holes?
ANSWER: They sell them to the Swiss cheese factory.

What does a worm do in a cornfield?
ANSWER: It goes in one ear and out the other.

What did the judge say when the skunk came before him?
ANSWER: Odor in the court!

What's worse than a giraffe with a sore throat?
ANSWER: A centipede with sore feet.

What do you call two spiders who just got married?
ANSWER: Newlywebs.

Why do you comb your hair before you go to bed?
ANSWER: To make a good impression on the pillow.

What has two legs but can't walk?
ANSWER: A pair of pants.

What goes ha ha thump?
ANSWER: Someone laughing his head off.

What's the kindest animal in the world?
ANSWER: A skunk; he'll always give you his last scent.

Why does a traffic signal turn red?
ANSWER: You'd turn red too if you had to change in front of all those people.

What has two holes and runs?
ANSWER: A nose.

Why did the house call the doctor?
ANSWER: It had a window pane.

Why is a baseball team like pancakes?
ANSWER: They both depend on the batter.

What belongs to you but is used mostly by other people?
ANSWER: Your name.

Why shouldn't you put the letter *M* in your refrigerator?
ANSWER: It would turn the ice into mice.

Why is the letter *F* like a cow's tail?
ANSWER: Because it's at the end of the beef.

Why did Humpty Dumpty have a great fall?
ANSWER: He wanted to make up for a bad summer.

How many men and women were born in the country last year?
ANSWER: None. Only babies were born.

How many ears of corn could you eat on an empty stomach?

ANSWER: Only one; after that your stomach isn't empty anymore.

What looks like half a cheese?
ANSWER: The other half.

How did the rocket lose its job?
ANSWER: It got fired.

What's the difference between here and there?
ANSWER: The letter *T*.

Where would you go to see a man eating fish?
ANSWER: A seafood restaurant.

What's green, has six legs, and can jump over your head?
ANSWER: A grasshopper with the hiccups.

Why did Santa use only seven reindeer?
ANSWER: He left Comet home to clean the sink.

What did the dog say when his owner asked him where the TV antenna repairman was?
ANSWER: "Roof, roof."

What did the dog say when he stepped on sandpaper?
ANSWER: "Ruff, ruff."

What did the dog say when he was introduced to Mr. Nader, the consumer advocate?
ANSWER: "Ralph, Ralph."

What can you change more often than you change your clothes?
ANSWER: Your mind.

What keys don't open doors?
ANSWER: Donkeys, monkeys, and turkeys.

Where do moths dance?
ANSWER: At a moth ball.

What question can never be truthfully answered "yes"?
ANSWER: Are you sleeping?

Why did the man chew gum on the train?
ANSWER: The train kept saying "choo-choo."

Where do cows go on dates?
ANSWER: To the m-o-o-o-o-o-vies.

What did Tennes-see?
ANSWER: The same thing Arkan-saw.

What's hard to beat?
ANSWER: A torn drum.

Who wrote, "Oh say, can you see?"
ANSWER: An eye doctor.

If you were shot at with a bow and arrow and the archer missed, what would that be?
ANSWER: An arrow escape.

What goes up and down but does not move?
ANSWER: A hill.

What did the girl owl say to her owl ex-boyfriend?
ANSWER: "I don't give a hoot about you."

What has a row of many teeth, is only a few inches long, and does not bite?
ANSWER: A comb.

How do you stop a dog from barking in the front seat of a car?
ANSWER: Put it in the back seat.

What animal do you look like when you go for a swim?
ANSWER: A little bear.

Why is a shopper like a baby just learning how to talk?
ANSWER: They both like to go buy-buy.

Why did the man call his car "baby"?
ANSWER: It never went anywhere without a rattle.

What's black and white, white and black, green-green, white, black and green, green, white and black.
ANSWER: Two skunks fighting over a pickle.

What would you do if you saw a big, hungry man-eating tiger?
ANSWER: Hope it didn't see you.

What did the record player say to the record?
ANSWER: "Hey, baby, wanta go for a spin?"

Why did the boy tiptoe past the medicine cabinet?
ANSWER: So he wouldn't wake the sleeping pills.

What has three feet but never walks?
ANSWER: A yardstick.

What's black when it's clean and white when it's dirty?
ANSWER: A chalkboard.

How do you flip cards into a hat?
ANSWER: Take your head out first.

Why did the turtle cross the road?
ANSWER: He wanted to get to a Shell station.

Why is the window shade business risky?
ANSWER: It has too many ups and downs.

What did the big chimney say to the little chimney?
ANSWER: "You're too young to smoke."

How do you make a strawberry shake?
ANSWER: Come up behind it and say BOO!

What's a hotel?
ANSWER: A place where you give up good dollars for bad quarters.

Why did the horn stop blowing?
ANSWER: Because it didn't give a hoot.

What does a crow do on the telephone?
ANSWER: It makes a phone caw.

There are twenty-six letters in the alphabet; take away one and how many do you have left?
ANSWER: Twenty-six; one is a number, not a letter.

What do you do if you break your arm in two places?
ANSWER: Don't go to those places again.

When does the teacher wear dark glasses?
ANSWER: When she has bright pupils.

The longer I live, the smaller I grow. You can stop what I am doing with just one blow. What am I?
ANSWER: A candle.

Why is the nose in the middle of the face?
ANSWER: Because it's the scenter.

What goes from house to house, but never moves?
ANSWER: A sidewalk.

What's the difference between an airplane passenger and a carpenter?

ANSWER: One boards a plane, and the other planes a board.

There are three houses—one red, one white, and one blue. The red house is on the northwest corner of an east–west street, the blue house is on the southeast corner of a north–south street. Where is the white house?
ANSWER: On Pennsylvania Avenue in Washington.

How do you pronounce the capitol of Missouri, Saint Louee or Saint Louis?
ANSWER: Jefferson City.

What do you get if you cross a turkey with a peach?
ANSWER: Peach gobbler.

What is a real-life drama that believes in cleanliness?
ANSWER: A soap opera.

What kind of fruit does an electric plant bear?
ANSWER: Currants.

What is the main ingredient in dog biscuits?
ANSWER: Collie flour.

Jokes in Verse

An apple dropping on his head
  Set Newton thinking, but—
The story might have been different
  Had it been a coconut.

There once was a lady named Perkins
Who simply doted on gherkins.
    In spite of advice,
    She ate so much spice,
She pickled her internal workin's.

    Little Jack Horner stood on a corner
Watching the girls go by.
    Along came a beauty; he yelled, "Hello cutie,"
And that's how he got his black eye.

A bird sat on a bookshelf
    And shook his head in doubt.
He wondered where those bookworms were
    He'd heard so much about.

When people tell me secrets
    I always want to ask,
"If you yourself can't keep them,
    Why give me the task?"

Mary had a watch.
    She swallowed it, it's gone.
Now everywhere that Mary goes,
    Time marches on.

It's hard to lose a friend
    When your heart is full of hope.

But it's worse to lose a towel
    When your eyes are full of soap.

Here I sit in the moonlight,
    Abandoned by women and men.
Murmuring over and over,
    "I'll never eat onions again."

I threw a pass into the air,
    It fell to earth, I know not where.
And that is why I sit and dream
    Upon the bench with the third-string team.

Pity the poor little firefly.
    He must have lost his mind.
To blunder through existence
    With his headlight on behind.

A green little chemist
    On a green little day,
Mixed some green little chemicals
    In a green little way.
The green little grasses
    Now tenderly wave
O'er the green little chemist's
    Green little grave.

Hickory, dickory, dock.
    The mouse ran up the clock.

He fell with a shock.
    It was an electric clock.

I often pause and wonder
    At fate's peculiar ways.
For nearly all our famous men
    Were born on holidays.

Hickory, dickory, dock.
    The mouse ran up the clock.
The clock struck one.
    The mouse escaped with minor injuries.

Roses are red.
    Violets are blue.
I can row a boat.
    Canoe?

There once was a boy named Geep,
Who would not go to sleep,
    But when his father said,
    "Get into that bed!"
From Geep was heard not a peep.

There once was a boy named Jim,
Who liked to fill the tub to the brim.
    When he tried to put in more
    It went on the floor
And Jim had to learn how to swim.

Little Willie was a chemist
  Little Willie is no more.
What he thought was H_2O
  Was H_2SO_4.

Star light, star bright,
  First star I've seen tonight,
I wish I may, I wish I might—
  —Oh, shucks, it's just a satellite.

School Days, School Days

DIANE: I spent ten hours over my math book last night.
HOMER: You did?
DIANE: Yes. It fell under my bed.

DIANE: What are you majoring in at college?
STEVE: Cycle-ology.
DIANE: Oh, so you're going to be a psychoanalyst.
STEVE: No, I'm going to repair bicycles.

TEACHER: Tom, name two pronouns.
TOM: Who, me?
TEACHER: That's correct.

TEACHER: Joe, give me the definition of a vacuum.
JOE (after thinking for a while, and pointing to his head): Gee whiz, I've got it up here, but I just can't explain it.

TEACHER: Were you copying the answer from your neighbor's paper?
STUDENT: Oh no, sir. I was just looking to see if he had mine right.

SCIENCE TEACHER: Now, this is a dogwood tree.
STUDENT: How can you tell?
SCIENCE TEACHER: Because of its bark.

A mother was very put out because the teacher insisted on a written excuse explaining her son's absence from school following a severe snowstorm. The mother sat down and dashed off the following note:

Dear Teacher:

Little Bobbie's legs are fourteen inches long. The snow was eighteen inches deep.

Very truly yours,
Bobbie's mother

TEACHER: A diamond is the hardest known substance. It will cut glass.
STUDENT: Glass! A diamond will even make an impression on a girl's heart.

TEACHER: When rain falls, does it ever rise again?
STUDENT: Yes. In dew time.

TEACHER: Who was Homer?
STUDENT: He was the fellow that Henry Aaron made famous.

Laugh and the class laughs with you, but you stay after school alone.

TEACHER: How many seasons are there?
STUDENT: Three—football, basketball, and baseball.

SCIENCE TEACHER: When do trees turn red?
STUDENT: In the autumn.
SCIENCE TEACHER: Why do they turn?
STUDENT: They're blushing to think how green they've been all summer.

TEACHER: Name a deadly poison.
STUDENT: Aviation.
TEACHER: Oh, don't be foolish.
STUDENT: Well, one drop is almost sure to kill.

MOTHER: Son, sit down and tell me what your school grades were.
SON: I can't sit down. I just told Dad what they were.

DOUG: Oh, shucks. I got a hundred in math today and still didn't pass.
MOTHER: Why not, for goodness' sake?
DOUG: The answer was two hundred.

TEACHER: Can any of you tell me of anything of importance that did not exist fifty years ago?
STUDENT: Me.

FATHER: I'm worried about your being at the bottom of your class.
SON: Don't worry about it. They teach the same thing at both ends.

DAD: If you had a little more spunk, you'd stand at the top of your class. Do you know what spunk is?
SON: Yes. It's the past participle of spank.

TEACHER: What is usually used as a conductor of electricity?
STUDENT: Why—er.
TEACHER: Correct, wire. Now, tell me the unit of electrical power.
STUDENT: The what?
TEACHER: Correct. The watt.

TEACHER: Can you tell me the shape of the world?
STUDENT: According to the latest reports, it's in terrible shape.

TEACHER: Here you see the skull of a chimpanzee of a very rare specimen. There are only two in this country. One is in the National Museum and I have the other.

TEACHER (to another teacher): Not only is Freddie the worst-behaved boy in school, but also he has a perfect attendance record.

Two boys were trying to define the word "collision."

"Collision," said one, "is when two things come together unexpectedly."

"I know," said the other. "Like twins."

TEACHER: How many senses did Nature give us?
STUDENT: Seven.
TEACHER: Name them.
STUDENT: Touch, sight, taste, smell, hearing, horse, and common.

TEACHER: Give an example of how science has helped business.
STUDENT: Look how the law of gravity has helped the sales of suspenders.

TEACHER: Max, tell us something about the Iron Age.
MAX: I'm sorry, teacher, but I'm a bit rusty on that subject.

TEACHER: Name a liquid that can't freeze.
STUDENT: Hot water.

TEACHER: If I gain four feet per second going down an incline, what will my condition be after twenty-five seconds?
STUDENT: You'll have become a centipede.

SCIENCE TEACHER: What happens when a body is immersed in water?
STUDENT: The telephone rings.

TEACHER: Let's take the example of the busy ant. He is busy all the time, works all day and every day. Then what happens?
STUDENT: He gets stepped on.

DOUG: What's the hurry?
DEENA: I bought a textbook and I'm trying to get to class before the next edition comes out.

A parent who wants his children to get an education these days may have to pull a few wires: the television wire, the stereo wire, and the radio wire.

TEACHER: Which is more important, the sun or the moon?
STUDENT: The moon.
TEACHER: Why do you say that?
STUDENT: The moon shines at night, when it's dark, but the sun shines in the day, when it's light anyway.

TEACHER (after a lesson on snow): As we walk out on a cold winter's day, what do we see on every hand?
STUDENT: Gloves.

Junior was being lectured about his poor grades. Little Harry, who lived a few doors away, was being held up as an example.

"Harry doesn't get Cs and Ds, does he?" asked Junior's father.

"No," Junior admitted. "But he has bright parents."

TEACHER: Will you students in the back of the room kindly stop passing notes?
STUDENT: We're not passing notes, teacher. We're playing poker.

TEACHER: Martha, tell me something about Christopher Columbus.
MARTHA: He was the explorer who discovered America, and he was very economical.
TEACHER: Economical?
MARTHA: Yes. He was the only man to travel three thousand miles on a galleon.

TEACHER: Kevin, spell mouse.
KEVIN: M-o-u-s.
TEACHER: But what's at the end of it?
KEVIN: A tail.

"My topic today," said the psychology teacher, "is the lie. How many of you have read the twenty-fifth chapter of the textbook?"

Nearly all of the students raised their hands.

"Good," said the teacher. "You're just the group I want to talk to. The textbook has only twenty-four chapters."

STAN: I'm not going to school any more.
MOTHER: Why?
STAN: On Monday the teacher said that four and four make eight. On Tuesday she said six and two make eight. Today she said seven and one are eight. I'm not going back to school until she makes up her mind.

SCIENCE TEACHER: What's the difference between electricity and lightning?
STUDENT: We have to pay for electricity.

TEACHER: What does HNO_3 mean?
STUDENT: It's right on the tip of my tongue.
TEACHER: Spit it out. It's nitric acid.

LITTLE BOY: That's my dad's signature on my excuse, Teacher, and here's the tracing to prove it.

TEACHER: Why are you late for school, Betty?
BETTY: There are nine children in our family, and the alarm was set for eight.

SON: What are five oranges plus three oranges?

FATHER: Add five oranges to three oranges? Don't you know the answer? Haven't you ever done a problem like this before?
SON: No. In school we added apples.

The teacher asked the class to list, in their own opinion, the eleven great Americans of today. After a while, she stopped at one desk and asked the student, "Have you finished your list yet?"

"Not yet," replied the student. "I just can't decide on the split end."

TERRY: I'm taking ancient history.
SHERRY: So am I. Let's get together and talk over old times.

TEACHER: Charlie, if I had two sandwiches and you had two sandwiches, what would we have?
CHARLIE: Lunch.

TEACHER: Suppose that the people on Mars sent us a message. How could they tell if we received it?
STUDENT: They could send it collect and see if we paid for it.

The teacher told the class to write a composition on baseball. One minute later,

Johnny turned in his paper. It read: "Game called on account of rain."

GLEN: Why are you taking your math to gym?
BEN: Because I have some fractions to reduce.

MOTHER: Danny's teacher says he ought to have an encyclopedia.
FATHER: Let him walk to school like I did.

DENNIS: Mother, will you do my arithmetic for me?
MOTHER: No, Dennis. It wouldn't be right.
DENNIS: Well, you could try.

TEACHER: Use "income" in a sentence.
MOE: I opened the door and income the cat.
TEACHER: Wrong. Try "ransom."
MOE: I saw a skunk and ransom distance away.
TEACHER: Try "handsome."
MOE: Handsome candy to me.
TEACHER: Your last chance is "gruesome."
MOE: Since last year I gruesome.

"Vinnie," said the teacher, "to what family does the whale belong?"
"I don't know," said Vinnie. "No one in our neighborhood has one."

Then there was the cross-eyed teacher who had no control over his pupils.

And the teacher who graded examinations so carefully that he flunked three students for making their periods upside down.

GERALD: Mom, we had an algebra test today—only five problems.
MOTHER: Good. How many did you miss?
GERALD: The first two and the last three.

FATHER (to son): It's too bad that they don't give a grade for courage. You would get an A for bringing this report card home.

ENGLISH TEACHER: What kind of punctuation would you use after this sentence: "A five-dollar bill was lying in the street"?
STUDENT: I'd make a dash after it.

Two boys were walking past a sign in front of a school and one said to the other: "What do you think PTA means?"
The other one said, "I think it means 'poor, tired adults.'"

WILLIE: Have you read any mystery books lately?

MAE: Yes. I'm right in the middle of one now.
WILLIE: What's it called?
MAE: Algebra.

TEACHER: Name the four seasons.
STUDENT: Salt, pepper, sugar, and spice.

TEACHER: Can anyone name a bird that is now extinct?
GRANT: Yes. Our canary. The cat extincted him last night.

FATHER: Well, son, how do you like school?
SON: Closed.

FATHER: Jimmy, how are your marks in school?
JIMMY: Underwater.
FATHER: What do you mean?
JIMMY: Below C level.

MRS. SMITH: Tell me, Mrs. Jones, how is your son doing in school?
MRS. JONES: Just fine. He's so accurate and thorough that he stays in every class for two years.

SMALL BOY (to his father): Here's my report card and one of yours that I found in the attic.

QUESTION: Why do kindergarten math teachers enjoy life so much?
ANSWER: They make the little things count.

PHYSICS TEACHER: Haven't you had pi in your math class?
STUDENT: No, but the teacher served us ice cream once.

STUDENT: I don't think that I deserved a zero on this paper.
TEACHER: Neither do I, but it's the lowest grade I can give.

SCIENCE TEACHER: Name three things that contain starch.
STUDENT: Two cuffs and a collar.

After a long lesson on teeth, the teacher asked, "Name three different kinds of teeth."
A student answered: "Temporary, permanent, and false."

ENGLISH TEACHER: Use a word ten times and it will be yours for life.
GIRL STUDENT: Joe, Joe, Joe, Joe, Joe, Joe, Joe, Joe, Joe, Joe.

FATHER: What's that very low number on your report card?

SON: Maybe it's the temperature of the schoolroom.

MATHEMATICS TEACHER: Now, if I lay three eggs here and lay five eggs over there, how many eggs will I have?
STUDENT: To tell you the truth, I don't think that you can do it.

TEACHER: If you had ten potatoes and wanted to divide them equally, how would you do it?
STUDENT: I'd mash them.

MAN: What are you doing in my lumberyard?
BOY: I'm looking for the board of education.

TEACHER: Why did you miss all the problems on your math paper?
STUDENT: To give credit where credit is due, I wouldn't have missed all the problems without the valuable assistance of my father.

FATHER: How are you doing in school this year?
SON: I'm as famous as Napoleon.
FATHER: How's that?
SON: I went down in history, too.

TEACHER: Does anyone know what cowhide is used for?
STUDENT: It holds the cow together.

TEACHER: Is it true, Andy, that lightning never strikes twice in the same place?
ANDY: Yes. When lightning strikes once, the same place isn't there any more.

TEACHER: Why are winter days shorter than summer days?
STUDENT: Because they expand when heated and contract when cooled.

A teacher, annoyed by his clock-watching students, covered the face of the clock with this sign: "Time will pass—will you?"

A young man had just gotten home from his first year at college and said to his father proudly: "Dad, did you know pi r square?"
His father flew into a rage and said, "That college is no good. Everyone knows that pies are round."

TEACHER: Where is the Red Sea?
STUDENT: On my report card.

TEACHER: Use the word "politics" in a sentence.
STUDENT: My parrot swallowed a watch and now Politics.

FATHER: What is the meaning of those Ds and Fs on your report card?
SON: Oh, Dad, that means I'm Doing Fine.

SCIENCE TEACHER: What is the fastest-burning substance known to man?
STUDENT: I don't know whether it's my allowance or the gas in my car.

FATHER: Why is your January report card marked so low?
SON: Well, you know how it is, Dad. After Christmas everything is marked down.

The little boy had just started to school. When he returned home the first day, his mother asked: "What did you learn?"
"I learned to write," he replied.
"What did you write?" asked the mother.
"How do I know?" said the boy. "I haven't learned to read yet."

Sitting in class with his friend, a boy said that he was very hungry. His friend said, "Just eat the textbook. It's full of baloney."

"Say, Mom," said Steve. "There's a special PTA meeting at school this afternoon."

"Really?" said his mother. "What's so special about that?"

"It's just for you," said Steve. "Oh yes, the principal, my teacher, and I have been invited, too."

TOM: Our teacher talks to himself, how about yours?

CATHY: My teacher does, too. When he talks to us, he thinks that we are listening.

TEACHER: Can you tell me how fast light travels?

STUDENT: No, but I know that it gets here too early in the morning.

A teacher asked her class to correct this sentence: "Girls is naturally more beautiful than boys."

One little boy wrote: "Girls is artificially more beautiful than boys."

CRAIG: You know, Stella, history does have a way of repeating itself.

STELLA: I know. I've failed it twice already.

SON: Dad, how do you find the least common denominator?

FATHER: Great Scott, haven't they found that thing yet? They were looking for it when I was in school.

TEACHER: Why don't you answer me?
STUDENT: I did. I shook my head.
TEACHER: You didn't expect me to hear it clear up here, did you?

CIVICS TEACHER: Who is the Speaker of the House?
STUDENT: Mother.

TEACHER: If your father had ten dollars and you asked him for two dollars and eighty-nine cents, how much would be left?
STUDENT: Ten dollars.
TEACHER: You don't know your math.
STUDENT: You don't know my father.

TEACHER: Who was the greatest inventor the world has ever known?
STUDENT: A man called Pat Pending.

MIRIAM: Walter, don't forget to record the results of this last step in our chemistry experiment. Now let's get these chemicals mixed.
WALTER (later): Miriam, how do you spell KABOOM!?

Craig's science teacher was disturbed because of his lack of progress in class. The teacher wrote a note home to Craig's parents. Craig's father was delighted with the note and told a friend that his boy was headed for a career as an astronaut.

"How do you know?" asked the friend.

The father said, "Because the teacher said in the letter that Craig was taking up space."

The teacher made a firm statement of what kind of work she expected. She closed her remarks by saying that it would take far more than a mere "apple for the teacher" to earn a passing grade.

Apparently she made her point, because the next morning one of the students gave her a watermelon.

ANNA MAE: What kind of marks did you get in physical education last semester?
DIRK: A few bruises.

DANA: I don't see any reason for washing my hands before school.
MOTHER: Why not?
DANA: I never raise them in class, anyway.

TEACHER: Where is the largest corn grown?
STUDENT: On my father's little toe.

MOTHER: What did you learn in school, Skip?
SKIP: Just gosinta.
MOTHER: What's gosinta?
SKIP: You know. Three gosinta nine, two gosinta twelve.

TEACHER: Go to the office and see if anyone is there.
STUDENT: Alright.
TEACHER (later): What did you find?
STUDENT: There's not a single person up there.
TEACHER: Are they all married?

TEACHER: Are the examination questions giving you any trouble?
STUDENT: No. The questions are clear. It's the answers that are giving me trouble.

TEACHER: Without oxygen, discovered in 1773, human life would be impossible.
STUDENT: What did people breathe before oxygen was discovered?

TEACHER: Let's suppose that I want to switch the electric light on and it doesn't work. What may be wrong?
STUDENT: Maybe you forgot to pay the bill.

TEACHER: How should you study so that you will learn the most?

STUDENT: Close one ear so that the information has to stop in the middle.

BERNIE: Joe was caught cheating on a test.
DONALD: What happened?
BERNIE: They saw him counting his ribs in a biology exam.

TEACHER: This gas is a deadly poison. What steps would you take if it escaped?
STUDENT: Long ones.

JOHN: It's easy for you to get straight As in French. You were born and brought up in Paris.
HARRIS: Oh yeah? If that's the way it works, then you should get straight As in geometry.
JOHN: Why do you say that?
HARRIS: Because you're a square, a blockhead, and you keep running around in circles.

MATH TEACHER: And so we find that X is equal to zero.
STUDENT: Gee. All that work for nothing.

TEACHER: We will have only a half day of school this morning.
CLASS: Hooray!
TEACHER: We'll have the other half this afternoon.

TEACHER: Goodness, haven't you finished washing that blackboard yet? You've been working on that for an hour.
STUDENT: I know. But the more I wash it, the blacker it gets.

BOY: My teacher was mad at me because I didn't know where the Great Lakes were.
FATHER: Next time remember where you put things.

STUDENT: I hear that fish is brain food.
ROOMMATE: Yes. I eat it all the time.
STUDENT: Another theory disproved.

TEACHER: What is one half of one tenth?
STUDENT: I don't know exactly, but it can't be very much.

A small boy scowling over his report card said to his father: "Naturally I seem stupid to my teacher. He's a college graduate."

TEACHER: What does N-E-W spell?
STUDENT: New.
TEACHER: What does N-E-W spell if I put a *K* in front of it?
STUDENT: Canoe.

TEACHER: Bill, why is it that everyone else has at least a five-page report on milk, and your composition is only a half page long?
BILL: I was writing about condensed milk.

TEACHER: You can't sleep in my class!
STUDENT: I could if you didn't talk so loudly.

For three nights the father had struggled to help his little daughter unravel the puzzling math problems she had been given for homework. They were not making much progress.

"Daddy, it's going to be even worse next week," she said.

"What happens next week?" the father asked.

"Next week," she said, "we start learning the dismal system."

GARY: I got two prizes in school.
TINA: What were they for?
GARY: One was for remembering things so well. I can't remember what the other thing was for.

XAVIER: Did you see the plant in the algebra teacher's room?
HORACE: No. What about it?
XAVIER: It's growing square roots.

TEACHER: How many fingers do you have?
STUDENT: Ten.
TEACHER: And if you took away four, what would you have?
STUDENT: No piano lessons.

TEACHER: Sam, when was Rome built?
SAM: It was built during the night.
TEACHER: Where did you get that idea?
SAM: Everybody knows that Rome wasn't built in a day.

TEACHER: Suppose your mother made a cherry pie and there were nine of you at the table. How much of the pie would you get?
STUDENT: One eighth of it.
TEACHER: No. Pay attention. There are nine of you. Don't you know your fractions?
STUDENT: Yes. But I know my mother, too. She's on a diet and can't eat pie.

TEACHER: Why are you crying, Janet?
JANET: I'm crying because school bores me and I have to stay here until I'm at least sixteen.
TEACHER: Don't let that bother you. I have to stay here until I'm sixty-five.

A college boy wrote his father: "I can't understand why you call yourself a kind parent.

You haven't mailed me a check in almost two months. What type of kindness do you call that?"

The father wrote back: "Unremitting kindness."

TEACHER: Did you know that Henry Hudson discovered the Hudson River?
STUDENT: What a coincidence.

MOTHER: If you don't go to school, the police will put your father and me in jail.
LITTLE BOY: For how long?

TEACHER: Why are you so late, Eddie?
EDDIE: Because of a sign by the road.
TEACHER: What does a sign have to do with being late?
EDDIE: The sign I saw said: "School Ahead, Slow Down."

TEACHER: Name three collective nouns.
STUDENT: The dustpan, the wastebasket, and the vacuum sweeper.

TEACHER: Frank, if you found three dollars in your right pocket and two dollars in your left pocket, what would you have?
FRANK: Somebody else's pants on.

TEACHER: Give me a sentence with an object.
STUDENT: You're very beautiful, teacher.
TEACHER: What's the object?
STUDENT: A good grade.

TEACHER: What three words do students use most?
STUDENT: I don't know.
TEACHER: Correct.

TEACHER: Is there any word in the English language that contains all the vowels?
STUDENT: Unquestionably.

ALBERT: Teacher, would you punish anyone for something he didn't do?
TEACHER: Certainly not.
ALBERT: Good, because I didn't do my homework.

SUNDAY SCHOOL TEACHER: Tommy, don't you want to go to heaven?
TOMMY: I better not. My mother told me to get right home after Sunday School.

TEACHER (on first day of school): What's your name, son?
STUDENT: Jule.
TEACHER: No, not Jule—Julius.
STUDENT: I like Jule.

TEACHER (sternly): As long as you are in my class your name is Julius.
STUDENT: OK.
TEACHER (to another student): And what's your name, young man?
SECOND STUDENT: Bilious.

JACK: Hooray! the teacher said we would have a test rain or shine!
JOAN: But that's nothing to be happy about.
JACK: It's snowing.

TEACHER: To a geologist, a thousand years is nothing.
STUDENT: Oh boy! Why did I lend my uncle the geologist ten dollars?!

TEACHER: Jerry, give me the formula for water.
JERRY: H, I, J, K, L, M, N, O.
TEACHER: What kind of a crazy answer is that?
JERRY: You told us water was H to O.

ODE TO AN UPPERCLASSMAN

You can tell a freshman
By his silly eager look.
You can tell a sophomore
Because he carries one less book.

You can tell a junior
By his dashing air and such.
You can tell a senior
But, boy, you can't tell him much!

SCHOOL SECRETARY (on the phone): You say Eric has a bad cold and can't come to school? Who is this speaking?
VOICE: This is my father.

COLLEGE STUDENT I: How do you keep your roommate from reading your mail?
COLLEGE STUDENT II: I hide the letters in his textbooks.

A politician was invited to give a speech at a school. He talked and talked for a long time, pausing only to look at his watch. He then said to the audience, "My watch has stopped. Does anyone have a watch?"

"No," said someone in the audience. "But there's a calendar behind you."

TEACHER: If you have five candy bars and gave away two of them, what would you have then?
STUDENT: Two new friends.

GAIL: I'm exhausted. I was up until midnight doing my homework.

NEIL: What time did you start?
GAIL: Eleven forty-five.

TEACHER: How much is nine and nine?
STUDENT: Ninety-nine.

TEACHER: Where is the English Channel?
STUDENT: I don't know. We can't get it on our TV.

TEACHER: This is the fifth day in a row this week you had to stay after school. What do you have to say for yourself?
STUDENT: Boy, am I glad it's Friday!

GLORIA: Dad, can you write in the dark?
FATHER: Certainly.
GLORIA: Great. Would you turn off the light and sign my report card?

The ticket seller at the movie theater looked suspiciously at the young boy who at one o'clock in the afternoon asked for a ticket.
"Shouldn't you be in school, young man?" she asked.
"It's OK," he said. "I have the measles."

TEACHER: Make up a sentence using the word "fascinate."

STUDENT: My coat has ten buttons, but I can only fasten eight.

For show and tell, the first grader was talking to the class about a thermometer.

"When the Jupiter goes up," said the boy, pointing to the thermometer, "it's hot; when it goes down, it's cold."

"You mean *mercury*," said the teacher.

"Oh, I guess I got my planets mixed up," said the boy.

MOM: How was school today?
CAROL: OK, I guess, except for the new teacher.
MOM: What's the matter with the new teacher?
CAROL: She doesn't keep her promises. She told me to sit in a new seat for the present, but she never did give me the present.

The nursery school teacher struggled to get one child's boots on one rainy day, but she was having a hard time. After she got them on, the little boy said, "These boots aren't mine."

"Then why did you let me put them on?" asked the teacher as she took them off.

"They're my brother's, but my mother lets me wear them," answered the boy.

TEACHER: Why is it when I come back into the room after being out for a while, I find that you're not working?

STUDENT: Because you have rubber heels and soles on your shoes.

A college student wrote this letter:
Dear Dad:
Gue$$ what I need mo$t. Plea$e $end it a$ $oon a$ you can.
Be$t wi$he$,
Your $on $tan

The father's reply:
Dear Son:
NOthing much is happening here. It sNOwed yesterday. We kNOw you must love college. Please write aNOther letter soon. Take good NOtes in your classes. I have to say good-by NOw.
Love, Dad

PEG: Is your brother going to be married?

MEG: I don't think so. He's going to get a bachelor's degree.

TEACHER: What is a synonym?

STUDENT: It's a word you use when you can't spell the other one.

TEACHER: Where's your pencil?
STUDENT: I ain't got one.
TEACHER: Don't say ain't. Listen. I don't have a pencil, he doesn't have a pencil, they don't have a pencil.
STUDENT: Gee, what happened to all of them?

TEACHER: Can you tell me the opposite of happiness?
OSCAR: Sadness.
TEACHER: Good. Can you tell me the opposite of sadness?
OSCAR: Gladness.
TEACHER: Very good. Now can you tell me the opposite of woe?
OSCAR: Giddap.

TEACHER: Why are you late, Louise?
LOUISE: I left home late.
TEACHER: Why didn't you leave home earlier?
LOUISE: By the time I left it was too late to start early.

TEACHER: Why is your homework paper so messy?
KIM: My pencil was in a hurry.

STAN: Isn't this the same arithmetic book we used last year?

JAN: It is, but it's OK, because Miss Hollis changed all the answers.

GLENN: Why did you hand in a perfectly clean, empty piece of paper for your English theme?
HARRIS: This time I wanted to be sure the teacher didn't take off any points for lack of neatness.

TEACHER: When water becomes ice, what is the greatest change that takes place?
STUDENT: The price.

Ed was having trouble pronouncing his Rs. Trying to help, the teacher gave him a sentence to read: "Robert gave Richard a rap in the ribs for roasting the rabbit so rare."
She told him to work on it for a few days. Later, when the teacher asked Ed to repeat the sentence he said, "Bob gave Dick a poke in the side for not cooking the bunny enough."

TEACHER: Define the word buoyant.
STUDENT: A male insect.

MOUNTAINEER (to son returning from college): What did you study in that there college, son?

SON: Biology, English, philosophy, and trigonometry.

MOUNTAINEER: I sure am glad you took some of that there triggernometry. You used to be the worst shot in the family.

MOM: Were you a good boy in school today?

SON: I certainly was. How much trouble can you get into standing in a corner all day?

All the kids were trying to impress Grandpa, who had come down for a visit. "I'm first in arithmetic," boasted Timmy. Sally said she had come in first in the spelling bee.

"What are you first in?" Grandpa asked of little Billy.

"Well, I'm first to be out of the door when the last bell rings."

TEACHER: What's farther away, the moon or China?

JEAN: China.

TEACHER: Why do you say that?

JEAN: Because you can see the moon but you can't see China.

The boy came home from school with a zero on his paper.

"Why did you get the zero?" his mother asked.

"That's no zero," the boy answered. "Teacher ran out of stars, so she gave me a moon."

TEACHER: I asked you to draw a horse and wagon. You've only drawn a horse.
STUDENT: I figured the horse would draw the wagon.

AUNT TILLIE: How do you like school?
LITTLE BILL: I like going, and I like coming back. It's the part in between I don't like.

TEACHER: Recite a sentence using the word "camphor."
STUDENT: I went to camphor a week.

TEACHER: Give me an example of wasted energy.
STUDENT: Telling a hair-raising story to a bald-headed man.

GARTH: I got an F on my history test, but it wasn't my fault.
MOTHER: Why not?
GARTH: The teacher asked me about things that happened before I was born.

TEACHER: I hope I didn't see you look at Hector's paper, Paul.
PAUL: I hope you didn't either, teacher.

CLARENCE: It's too bad Lincoln wasn't born in Nebraska.

LINDA: Why do you say that?

CLARENCE: That's what I put down on my history test.

Daffynitions

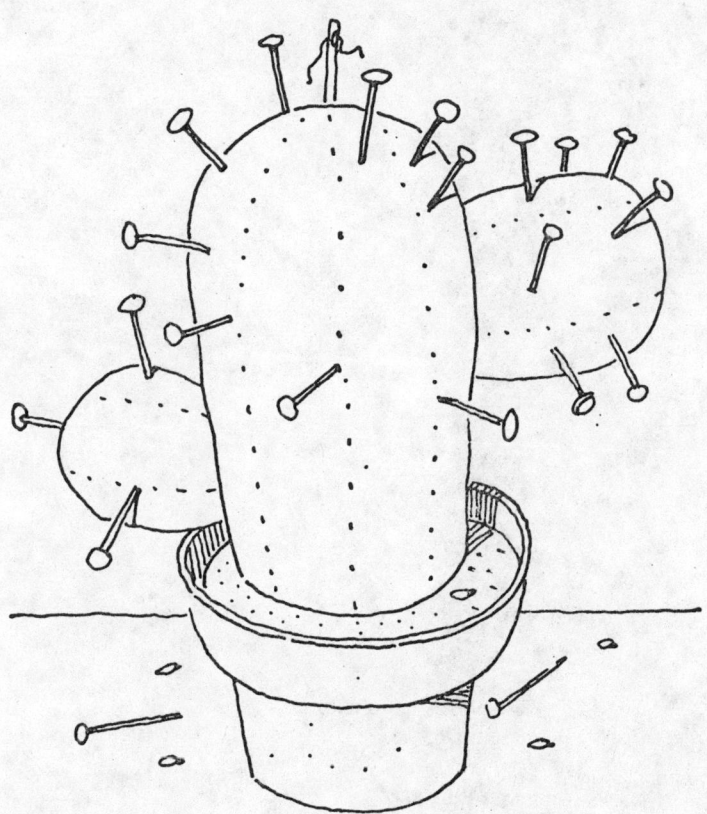

Cactus—An overgrown pincushion.

Tricycle—A tot rod.

Tomorrow—The great labor-saving device of today.

Conference—Meeting of the bored.

Hatchet—What a hen does to an egg.

Mosquito—A flying hypodermic needle.

Diploma—The guy who fixes the pipes.

Psychiatrist—A person who doesn't have to worry as long as other people do.

Satellite—What the modern cowboy puts on his saddle for nighttime riding.

Sundial—An old timer.

Hypodermic needle—A sick shooter.

Water cooler—A thirst aid kit.

Split second—The time from the point the light turns green to when the driver behind you blows the horn.

Research—When you look for something twice.

Frigidaire—A person who made a cool million.

Square meals—What too much of makes a person round.

Vitamin—What you do when someone comes to the house.

Raisin—A worried grape.

Unaware—The last thing to be taken off before you take a shower.

Laughingstock—Cattle with a sense of humor.

Erosion—The great terrain robbery.

Hair—Ear-to-ear carpeting.

Fission—A fine water sport.

After-dinner mint—What you need after the waiter hands you the check.

Soda jerk—A fizzician.

Singing—A man's bathright.

Egotist—A person who suffers from "I" strain.

Sole searcher—A fortune-teller who reads feet instead of palms.

Dimple—An inside-out bump.

Mountain climber—Someone who wants to take another peak.

Counterfeit money—Homemade bread.

Plateau—A disappointed mountain.

Fjord—A Norwegian car.

Camelot—Where you park your camel.

Autobiography—A history of automobiles.

Dust—Mud with the juice squeezed out.

Volcano—A mountain that blows its top.

Ice—Water that stayed out in the cold and went to sleep.

Bacteria—The rear entrance to the cafeteria.

Pedestrian—A person who thought there was a little gas left in the tank when the gauge read empty.

Skunk—A two-toned kitty with an exhaust pipe.

Climate—What kids do when they see a tree.

Horse sense—Stable thinking.

Illegal—A sick bird.

Shrunken head—A dehydrated noodle.

Coincide—What you should do when it starts to rain.

Jaywalking—An exercise that can give you that run-down feeling.

Earthquake—Mother Nature doing the twist.

Parking space—A space five inches too short on the other side of the street.

Generally—Famous commander of the Confederate Army.

Atom—A guy who went around with Eve.

Depth—Height turned upside down.

Jumping to conclusions—Skydiving without a parachute.

Vacation—Two weeks off followed by two off weeks.

Ohm—An Englishman's 'ouse.

Homework—Skulldrudgery.

The Wheels of Commerce

Including that all-time favorite—the fly in the soup

CUSTOMER: Waiter, there's a fly in my soup!
WAITER: There's no extra charge for the fly, sir.

A laundry advertized: "We don't mangle your clothes with our machinery. We do it carefully by hand."

DINER: Waiter, these beans seem rather stringy.
WAITER: Maybe it would help, madam, if you removed your veil.

GAS STATION ATTENDANT to OLD CAR OWNER: Your oil's OK, but your engine needs changing.

CUSTOMER: How much is a cup of coffee?
WAITRESS: Fifty cents.
CUSTOMER: How much is the refill?
WAITRESS: It's free.
CUSTOMER: Good. I'll just take the refill.

WAITER: How did you find your steak, sir?
DINER: Just by accident. I moved the boiled potato and there it was.

MAN IN RESTAURANT: I'll have a couple of lamb chops, and make them lean, please.
WAITER: To which side?

LAWYER: When I was a boy, my ambition was to become a pirate.
CLIENT: Congratulations.

Sign in a restaurant window: "T-Bone Steak, $1.00."

Then, in fine print underneath: "With Meat, $12.00."

LADY IN JEWELRY STORE: Can you appraise my sapphire? And, while you're at it, tell me the correct way to spell it?

JEWELER: G-L-A-S-S.

The vacuum cleaner salesman was illustrating his sales talk by repeatedly sprinkling sand on the rug and removing the sand very deftly with his vacuum cleaner.

"Now, madam," he wound up, turning to one woman in the crowd around him, "can I interest you in buying one of our vacuum cleaners?"

"No good to us," was the reply. "We never sprinkle sand on our rugs."

SALESMAN: This model has a top speed of one hundred thirty miles an hour, and she'll stop on a dime.

PROSPECT: What happens after that?

SALESMAN: A little putty knife comes out and scrapes you off the windshield.

The motorist and the garage attendant had different ideas about what ailed the old car.

"This happens to be my car," said the

motorist. "And I'll have you know that what I say about it goes."

"OK," growled the attendant. "Try saying 'engine.'"

A parrot was being sold at an auction and offers for the bird mounted rapidly. Finally, after a fiercely competitive few minutes, one of the bidders won out.

"Can this bird talk?" he asked the auctioneer.

"I'll say he can," came the answer. "Who do you think was bidding against you?"

Sign in a service station: "We collect taxes—federal, state, and local. We also sell gasoline as a sideline."

Newspaper ad: "Car for sale: First-Crash Condition."

STORE CLERK: I suppose this pen is going to be a surprise present.

CUSTOMER: It certainly is. It's for my son who's graduating. He's expecting a motorcycle.

The motorist drove his long, powerful car into a filling station and ordered the attendant to fill it up. After a while the attendant said: "Better turn off the engine. You're gaining on me."

WIFE: How many fish did you catch on your outing?
HUSBAND: Six.
WIFE: Well, then, the market made a mistake. They charged us for eight.

CUSTOMER: I want to buy a dog. How much are these?
CLERK: They're five dollars apiece.
CUSTOMER: Oh, but I want a whole one.

Then there was the man who bought a sack of mothballs and the next day brought them back to the drugstore. "These things are no good," he said. "I sat up all night throwing them at the blasted moths and didn't hit a single one."

TAILOR: Would you like to try on the suit in the window?
CUSTOMER: If it's alright with you, I'd rather use the dressing room.

MOTHER: What do you say to the nice grocer for giving you a piece of cake?
CHILD: Charge it.

TENANT: It rained last night and the water came through the roof and gave me a shower bath. Aren't you going to do anything about it?

LANDLORD: What do you expect me to do, give you a towel and some soap?

PASSENGER: I'm afraid that my dog has eaten my ticket.
CONDUCTOR: Then I would suggest that you buy him another helping.

A taxi drove up to an apartment building. A lady approached the vehicle, but it drove away before she could get in. The woman said: "That's what I call a Yellow Cab."

WAITER: Would you like black coffee?
CUSTOMER: What other colors do you have?

MAN: My hair is coming out pretty fast. Can't you give me something to keep it in?
BARBER: Sure. Take this shoe box.

CLERK: There you are, sir. That hat fits perfectly. How does it feel?
CUSTOMER: Fine, unless my ears get tired.

A man went into a fancy restaurant and ordered Poulet à la Maserati. It turned out to be a chicken that had been run over by an Italian sports car.

FUSSY CUSTOMER: Just look at this chicken you served me. One leg is longer than the other.
WAITER: Were you planning to eat it or dance with it?

AUDREY: My mother bought a genuine squirrel coat.
CHERYL: How can you tell?
AUDREY: She found nuts in the pocket.

CUSTOMER: Are bacon and eggs on your menu?
WAITER: No. We clean our menus regularly.

A man went into a pet shop to buy a singing canary. After a few minutes he bought one and left. The next day he returned and said, "When I got home, I saw that this canary had only one leg."

"Well," replied the owner, "you asked for a singer, not a dancer."

SHOPPER: Give me a mouse trap quickly, please. I have to catch a train.
CLERK: Sorry. We don't have any that big.

BOY: Do you have pop in the bottle?
GROCER: Yes.
BOY: Then let him out. My mother is calling him.

CUSTOMER: Can I wear this fur in the rain without hurting it?
SALESCLERK: Madam, have you ever seen a skunk carrying an umbrella?

HOTEL GUEST: The room is quite nice, but this wall is too thin. The people in the next room can hear everything I say.
HOTEL MANAGER: Well, to accommodate you, madam, we shall be pleased to hang a heavy tapestry on the wall.
HOTEL GUEST: But then I won't be able to hear what the people next door are saying.

CUSTOMER: I'll take five of those fish. Throw them to me.
STOREKEEPER: Why?
CUSTOMER: So I can tell everybody that I caught them.

"Don't you have any recent books on anatomy?" asked the young medical student. "These are at least twenty years old."
"Young man," said the librarian, "there haven't been any new bones added to the human body in that time."

CUSTOMER: May I have some birdseed?
GROCER: What kind of birds do you have?

CUSTOMER: I don't have any birds. That's why I want the birdseed. I want to grow one.

SHOPPER: How much are your eggs?
GROCER: Eighty cents a dozen for the good eggs and fifty cents a dozen for the cracked eggs.
SHOPPER: Good. Crack me a dozen.

PASSENGER: Is this my train?
CONDUCTOR: No. It belongs to the railroad.
PASSENGER: Don't be funny. Can I take this train to New York?
CONDUCTOR: No. It's much too heavy.

DINER: Waiter, I still haven't got that turtle soup that I ordered.
WAITER: Sorry. But you know how slow turtles are.

WAITER: Since you didn't eat your soup, I won't charge you for it.
MOTEL GUEST: Oh, by the way, I didn't sleep last night, either.

CUSTOMER: Waiter, I ordered an egg sandwich and you brought me a chicken sandwich.
WAITER: Sorry. I was a little late calling for your order.

SALESMAN: I'd like to have a few minutes of your time, if I may.

EXECUTIVE: Young man, my time is worth a hundred dollars an hour. However, I'll give you ten minutes.

SALESMAN: In that case, sir, if it's just the same to you, I'll take it in cash.

AUTO DEALER: This is a car that will pay for itself.

CUSTOMER: Well, as soon as it does, deliver it to me.

On the outskirts of a desert town are six service stations in a row. Posted in front of the first one is this sign: "Last chance to buy gas. The next five stations are mirages."

CUSTOMER: That chicken I bought yesterday had no wishbone.

BUTCHER: But it was a happy, contented chicken and had nothing to wish for.

DINER: Waiter, there's not a single split pea in my split pea soup.

WAITER: Well, did you ever see a devil in your devil's food cake?

Sign in a butcher shop: "Honest scales. No two weighs about it."

CUSTOMER: Give me some acetylsalicylic acid.
DRUGGIST: Do you mean aspirin?
CUSTOMER: Yes. I never can remember that name.

A man bought a parrot that could speak five languages for one thousand dollars. The pet shop owner said that he would deliver the bird that afternoon.

When the proud owner got home, he asked his wife if the parrot had been delivered. "Yes," she answered.

"Where is it?" he asked.

"In the oven," she answered.

"In the oven? But he could speak five languages."

"Well," asked his wife, "why didn't he speak up?"

A man went into a delicatessen to buy a pickle. The storekeeper reached into the pickle barrel with a dirty hand, threw the pickle onto a filthy piece of newspaper, wrapped it up, and handed it to the customer.

"I won't take that pickle," complained the customer, "this place is filthy. I surely won't come in here again until you clean it up."

A few months later the customer walked by the delicatessen again. It had a new front, clean windows, and fresh paint. He walked in and found the place sparkling clean, absolutely spotless. He said to the owner, "I see you cleaned the place up. How do you get a pickle now?"

"With the fork," said the owner, holding up a large stainless steel fork.

"Great. I'll take one," said the customer.

"I'm so clean," continued the owner as he speared a pickle, "that I don't even touch the handkerchief when I blow my nose."

"How do you do that?" asked the customer.

"See, the handkerchief is in my breast pocket. There's a string tied to the handkerchief. The string is looped over a pole running just under the ceiling. When I want to blow my nose I pull the string and that brings the handkerchief to my nose."

"Great," said the customer. "How do you get the handkerchief back into your pocket?"

"With the fork," answered the owner.

GENTLEMAN: Is your corn plaster any good?
PEDDLER: An infallible cure.
GENTLEMAN: Then give me a box. I'm going on a walking excursion tomorrow.
PEDDLER: Then take your umbrella. It's going to rain.
GENTLEMAN: How do you know?
PEDDLER: I can feel it in my corns.

CUSTOMER: I want a hamburger. Will it be long?
WAITER: No. It will be round, as usual.

TEEN-AGE GIRL to SALESWOMAN: I'm really crazy about this dress. But if my mother likes it, can I bring it back?

LANA: Go see if the chef has pigs' feet.
ALAN: OK.
LANA: Well, did he have pigs' feet?
ALAN: I don't know. He wouldn't take off his shoes.

BOOKSTORE CLERK: This book will do half your work for you.
CUSTOMER: Good. Give me two.

CAR DEALER to PARTNER: That smart-aleck foreign car dealer in town claims his cars are so easy on gas that they run off the fumes from our cars.

SHOPPER: How much are these tomatoes?
GROCER: Seventy cents a pound.
SHOPPER: Did you raise them yourself?
GROCER: Yes, I did. They were only sixty cents a pound yesterday.

CUSTOMER: I would like one pair of alligator shoes.
CLERK: Alright. What size does your alligator wear?

FORTUNE-TELLER: Can I help you?
BOY: Yes. How much would it cost to ask you two questions?
FORTUNE-TELLER: Five dollars.
BOY: Don't you think that that is a little high?
FORTUNE-TELLER: No. What's your second question?

Two astronauts opened the first restaurant on the moon. The food was good, but the restaurant lacked atmosphere.

JAN: Is this a second-hand store?
OWNER: Yes, it is.
JAN: Good. I need a new second hand for my watch.

There was the lady with laryngitis who went into the ice cream parlor.
LADY: What flavors do you have?
CLERK (in hoarse voice): Chocolate, vanilla, strawberry, buttercrunch, pistachio . . .
LADY: Oh. Do you have laryngitis too?
CLERK: No, lady, only the flavors I named.

YOUNG MAN: Do you have a card that says, "You're the only one I will ever love"?
CLERK: Yes, we do.
YOUNG MAN: Good, I'll take a dozen.

PET SHOP CUSTOMER: Is that bird for sale?
CLERK: Yes it is.
CUSTOMER: I'll take it. Can you send me the bill?
CLERK: Sorry, you'll have to take the whole bird or nothing at all.

CUSTOMER: How much is a haircut?
BARBER: Four dollars.
CUSTOMER: How much is a shave?
BARBER: A dollar and a half.
CUSTOMER: OK, shave my hair.

UNHAPPY CUSTOMER: When I bought this cat you said she was good for mice. She doesn't go near the mice!
PET SHOP OWNER: Well, isn't that good for the mice?

DINER: Do you serve crabs here?
WAITER: We serve anybody. Sit down.

A little boy watched as the shoe repairman repaired his shoes.

"What do you repair shoes with?" asked the boy.

"Hide," the repairman answered.

"What?" asked the boy.

"I said hide," the man repeated.

"Why?" the boy asked.

"Hide! Hide! The cow's outside," the man shouted impatiently.

"Who cares," answered the boy. "I'm not afraid of an old cow."

CUSTOMER: I'd like to buy a thermometer.
CLERK: What kind, Fahrenheit or Celsius?
CUSTOMER: Fahrenheit. I heard that's the better brand.

CUSTOMER: Waiter, why are there pennies in my soup?
WAITER: You said you would stop eating here unless there was some change in the food.

CUSTOMER: I want to return this cottage cheese. It has a splinter in it.
GROCER: What do you expect for the price of a little cottage cheese, a whole cottage?

CAR SALESMAN: I just delivered your new car to your door.
CUSTOMER: I know. I can hear it knocking.

WAITER: Shall I cut your pizza into six or twelve pieces?
CUSTOMER: Only six, please. I couldn't possibly eat twelve pieces.

ICE CREAM PARLOR CUSTOMER: I'll have a double chocolate fudge sundae with whipped cream, nuts, and candy sprinkles.
COUNTERPERSON: Shall I put a cherry on it?
CUSTOMER: Goodness no, I'm on a diet!

A merchant sent an overdue bill to a customer, attaching a note that read, "This bill is one year old today."
The customer sent the bill back with another note, which read, "Happy Birthday."

A teen-ager drove into a gasoline station in his broken-down car and asked for a quart of gasoline and a half-pint of oil. The attendant answered, "Do you want me to sneeze into your tires too?"

SALESMAN: I've been trying to see you for two weeks. May I have an appointment?
EXECUTIVE: Make a date with my secretary.
SALESMAN: I did that, but I still want to see you.

YOUNG MAN: I'd like to buy a box of pencils, please.
CLERK: Hard or soft?
YOUNG MAN: Soft. They're for writing love letters.

PET SHOP CUSTOMER: I'd take this dog, but its legs are too short.
CLERK: I don't think so, they reach right down to the floor.

MECHANIC: I found what was wrong with your car. You have a short circuit.
DRIVER: Good. Do whatever you have to do to lengthen it.

The label on the box said, "Money returned if not satisfactory." So the unhappy customer returned the product. A few weeks later he received a letter from the company. It read: "The money you paid for the product is entirely satisfactory; therefore, we are not returning it."

HARDWARE STORE CUSTOMER: I need some nails.
CLERK: What size, threepenny, sixpenny, ninepenny?
CUSTOMER: I want this job to be right, so I better take the kind that cost the most pennies.

BOY (in bakery): My mother says there was a fly in the raisin bread.

BAKER: Tell your mother to bring me the fly and I'll give her a raisin.

YOUNG MAN IN NEED OF A HAIRCUT: Are you the barber who cut my hair last time?

BARBER: Couldn't be. I've only been here two years.

The music store owner was so wrapped up in music that he put the following sign on his door: "Gone Chopin; be Bach later."

CHARLEY: My mother sent me to get a package of diapers for my little sister.

CLERK: Here you are. That will be three ninety-five for the diapers plus twenty cents for the tax.

CHARLEY: We don't need the tacks, we use safety pins.

WAITER: Have you tried the meatballs, sir?

CUSTOMER: Yes, and I found them guilty.

CUSTOMER: This soup isn't fit for a pig!

WAITER: Then I will bring you some that is, sir.

CUSTOMER: Could I put this wallpaper on myself?
CLERK: Certainly, but it would look better on a wall.

FATHER: Everything is going up, the price of food, clothing, automobiles, everything.
SON: Would you give me a new bicycle if I showed you something that's gone down?
FATHER: Yes!
SON: Here it is, my report card.

A large aardvark walked into an ice cream store and ordered an ice cream cone. The cone cost forty cents and the aardvark gave the clerk a five-dollar bill. The clerk thought the aardvark couldn't know much about money, so he gave the animal one dollar in change.

"We don't get many aardvarks in here," said the clerk as he gave the animal his change.

"I shouldn't wonder," said the aardvark, "at four bucks for a lousy ice cream cone."

The sign over the sandwich store said in large red letters: "WE MAKE ANY KIND OF SANDWICH IN THE WORLD."

A jokester walked in and asked, "Do you have elephant sandwiches?"

"How many elephant sandwiches do you want?" asked the counterman.

"One," answered the customer.

"On white, rye, or a hard roll?" asked the counterman.

"Rye."

"OK," said the counterman, "that will be $85,534.76 with tax."

"What!" screamed the customer. "Why so much?"

"Don't you know," replied the counterman, "that for your one lousy sandwich we got to buy and kill a whole elephant?"

WAITER: May I help you with your soup?
CUSTOMER: Why do you think I need help?
WAITER: From the sound of things I thought you needed to be dragged ashore.

WAITER: We have just about everything on our menu, sir.
CUSTOMER: I can see that. Why don't you bring me a clean one?

IRATE CUSTOMER: Waiter, there's a twig in my soup.
WAITER: I wouldn't be surprised, sir. This restaurant has branches all over the city.

CUSTOMER: Do you charge for bread in this restaurant?
WAITER: No.

CUSTOMER: Do you charge for gravy?
WAITER: No.
CUSTOMER: Good. I'll take bread and gravy.

DINER: I can't eat this food. Call the manager.
WAITER: It's no use. He can't eat it, either.

A lady went into a butcher shop and asked the man for a side of beef. The butcher went into the back room, brought out a cow, and said, "Which side, lady?"

WOMAN: What grade eggs do you have?
GROCER: First grade, second grade, and third grade.
WOMAN: Well, I want some that have graduated.

CUSTOMER: Waiter, there's a dead fly in my soup!
WAITER: It's the heat that kills them, sir.

CUSTOMER: Waiter, what's this fly doing in my soup?
WAITER: Looks like the backstroke.

CUSTOMER: Waiter, there's a fly drowning in my soup!
WAITER: Quick! give him mouth-to-mouth resuscitation, maybe we can save him!

CUSTOMER: Waiter, there's a fly in my black bean soup!

WAITER: Very well, sir. I'll take it to the chef and he'll exchange it for a bean.

CUSTOMER: Waiter, there's a fly in my soup!

WAITER (looking closely at the fly): Oh yes. His swimming is much better than it was yesterday.

CUSTOMER: Waiter, there's a fly in my soup.

WAITER: Don't worry about it. He won't eat too much.

Elephants Bringing Up the Rear

What would you get if you crossed an elephant with a groundhog?
ANSWER: I don't know, but you'd have a pretty big hole in your yard.

HANK: Why does an elephant have a trunk?
LINK: I don't know.
HANK: He would look pretty silly with a glove compartment.

HE: What do you find between elephants' toes?
SHE: Slow-running people.

TERRY: I wish I had enough money to buy an elephant.
KEN: Why do you want an elephant?
TERRY: I don't. I want the money.

How does an elephant get down from a tree?
ANSWER: He sits on a leaf and waits until fall.

What is gray on the inside and clear on the outside?
ANSWER: An elephant in a baggie.

ANN: Why do elephants paint their toes green and purple?
STAN: I don't know. Why?
ANN: So they can hide in the cookie jar.
STAN: That's silly. I've never seen an elephant in a cookie jar.
ANN: See. It works!

What's as big as an elephant but doesn't weigh an ounce?
ANSWER: An elephant's shadow.

Why does an elephant never forget?
ANSWER: What has he got to remember?

YOLANDA: What's the difference between a lemon, an elephant, and a tube of glue?
DIANE: I give up.
YOLANDA: You can squeeze a lemon, but you can't squeeze an elephant.
DIANE: What about the tube of glue?
YOLANDA: That's where you got stuck.

How do you stop an elephant from charging?
ANSWER: Take away his credit cards.

SUE: What does an elephant do when he has a broken toe?
NANCY: I don't know.
SUE: He calls a tow truck.

Why did the elephant eat a mothball?
ANSWER: To keep the moths out of his trunk.

Why did the elephant cross the road with a banana peel on her head?

ANSWER: She heard that blondes have more fun.

Why does an elephant paint its feet green?
ANSWER: So it can get across a pool table without being seen.

What time is it when an elephant sits on the fence?
ANSWER: Time to get a new fence.

Why was the elephant the last animal to get on the circus train?
ANSWER: It took him a long time to pack his trunk.

What's gray and yellow, gray and yellow, gray and yellow?
ANSWER: An elephant rolling down a hill with a daisy in its mouth.

How do you make an elephant float?
ANSWER: Put two scoops of ice cream, some milk, and soda water in a glass. Add one elephant.

BEN: I know a baby that gained ten pounds in three days from drinking elephant's milk.

CARLA: That's something. Whose baby was that?
BEN: The elephant's.

How do you fit six elephants in your car?
ANSWER: Put three in the front seat and three in the back seat.